AF317004

Caught in a Cat Romance

by Airie McCready

Library of Congress Control Number: 2025911531

Printed in La Vergne, Tennessee, United States of America

ISBN 979-8-9917290-2-4 (Paperback)
ISBN 979-8-9917290-3-1 (Hardcover)

Written, Illustrated and Edited by Airie McCready
Photography by Airie McCready and Jeff Bray
Formatted by Mandy L. Parrey

For rights and permissions, contact the publisher at:
Aber Stoat Publishing, LLC
2173 Salk Ave, Ste 250
Carlsbad, CA. 92008

hello@aberstoatpublishing.com
http://aberstoatpublishing.com
@aberstoat

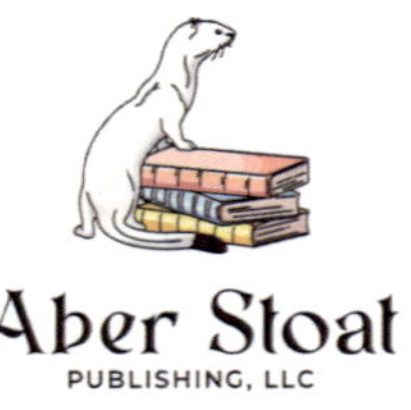

Aber Stoat
PUBLISHING, LLC

Dedication

This book is dedicated to my brother Matthew, who helped me through the hardest time in my life.

To my Father, a pillar of ethics in my world. I always knew he would choose the "right" way for all. He admired cats for their tenacity. He is my guardian angel, always looking over my shoulder.

To my first cat, Leo, who is always on my father's shoulder, helping him.

Table of Contents

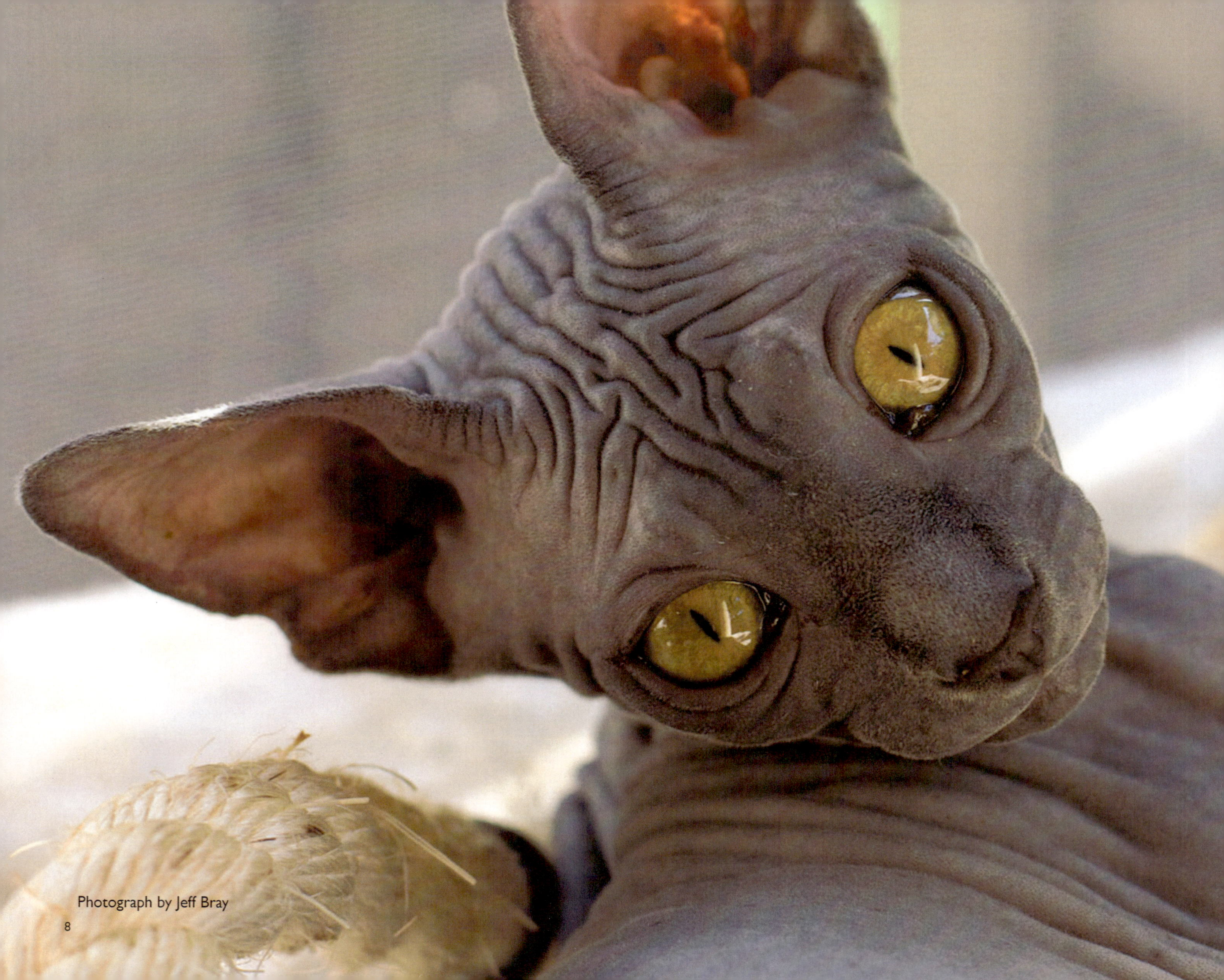

Photograph by Jeff Bray

Magical

Magical you walk and talk,
magical you play.
   Sing a little magic spell,
   what's that that you say?
Twirling with a little ball,
leaping high with glee.
   Running up the wall and then,
   running straight up me!
Run and jump and POP right up,
at nothing I see there.
   Invisible birds, mice & bugs,
   then attacking my long hair!
Chewing on my blue jeans,
Stealing all my shoes,
   My little naked kitten-cat,
   you drive away my blues!
Conjuring a happy spell,
Alchemist of my heart.
   May I keep you close to me,
   and may we never part.

Photograph
by Jeff Bray

You Love, I Love You

Tonight my bed's like a sanded shore,
where naked sun worshipers have come to snore.
Strewn about, legs out long, tails limp and relaxed,
they dream - smacking lips - of delicious cat snacks.

As the warmth fills them up from above and below,
their content little noises now ebb and flow.
The longer they lay, the further they stretch,
toes twitching as they dream
of long games of fetch.

Now I can get close, feel their breath, see them glow,
full fell of radiance and love that they know.
I brought them in hoping for unconditional love-
now they let me love them
and that's more than enough.

The lesson is backwards, the teacher to learn,
the student is me, and for their knowledge I yearn.
How do they do it, how do they just be?
in the moment, in the minute,
I wish I could see.

While my giving is love, their taking is too,
now they open their eyes of yellow and blue.
I know now that they love me,
of that I'm aware
Now they let me love them,
it glows in their stare.

Art by Airie McCready

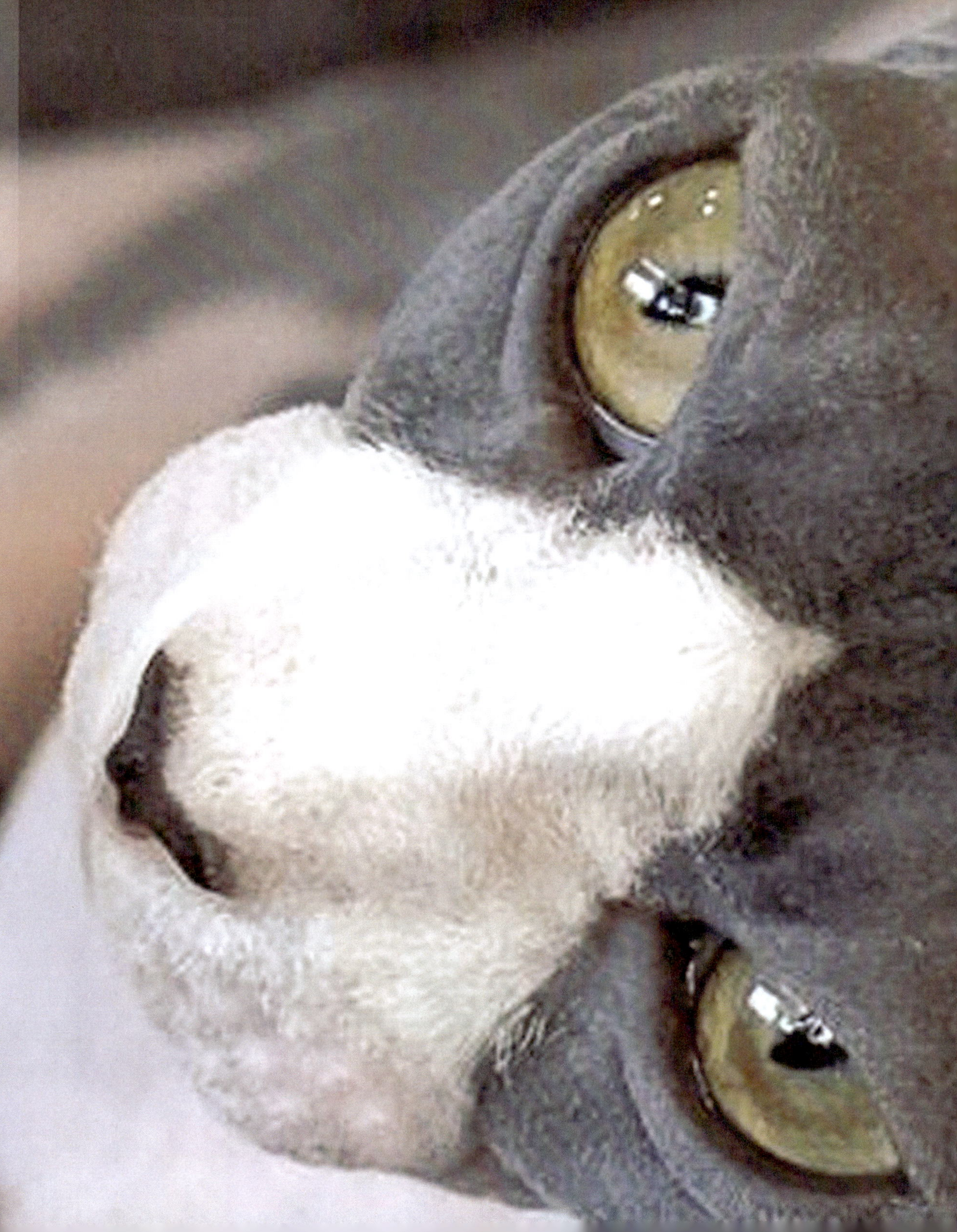
Perfect

My finger traces your velvet skin
where the day leaves off
and the dreams begin.
Your little hoofbeats run down the hall,
such loud noises from feet so small.
Tales of creatures that seem like you,
were only in books that I ever knew.
When I was little I wanted a Unicorn-
I did not know you were already born.
Sometimes you fly, sometimes you fall,
such a lion's heart in one so small.
You make me laugh, you make me sing,
You're a little queen, a miniature king.
You rule my heart, my little minx
that someone bred-
and named you Sphynx.

Photograph by Jeff Bray

Someone Once Found Beauty There

Little one that walks on clouds, gently with a cushioned tread.
leaps steady and without a sound, comes gliding up upon my bed.

As I lay in fitful sleep, and toss and sweat the night away,
she watches and without a sound, gently takes my pain away.

My tiny lover's velvet skin, nestles close to my fevered cheek
and in my sleep I settle down, feeling somehow not so weak.

She lays her face down close to mine, tiny nose, no whiskers there,
and sings to me a song of time, of love that happens with no hair.

My little creature comforts me, she makes me sing, she makes me sigh,
and I thank the ones who brought her here, who saw a cat with a different eye.

A thing that might seem odd and wrong, that looked as ancient as a crone,
someone once found beauty there, and now I'll never be alone.

When I awake I gaze at her, she is the landscape, she is all I see
I'd move the heavens and the earth to keep my angel close by me.

I know one day she will go on, over a bridge with rainbow flare.
My little bird, my little muse, it will be too long till I meet you there.

So now I hold you close and laugh, my little one, such joy, such tears
of happiness run down my cheeks, and you lick them away with all my fears.

There are so many who are sad, and angry in this world it seems-
think of the peace and love and joy - if everyone was loved by a sphynx.

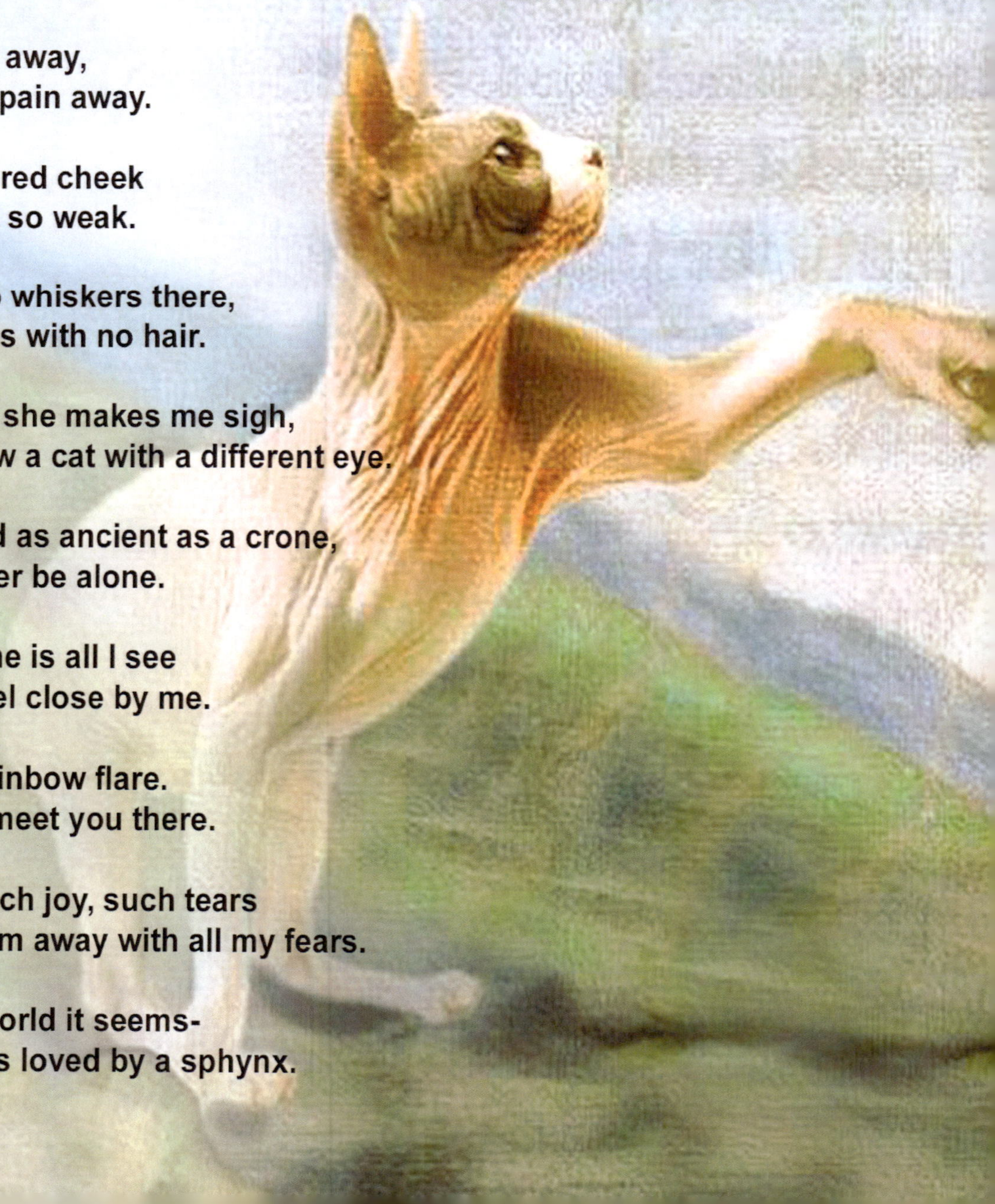

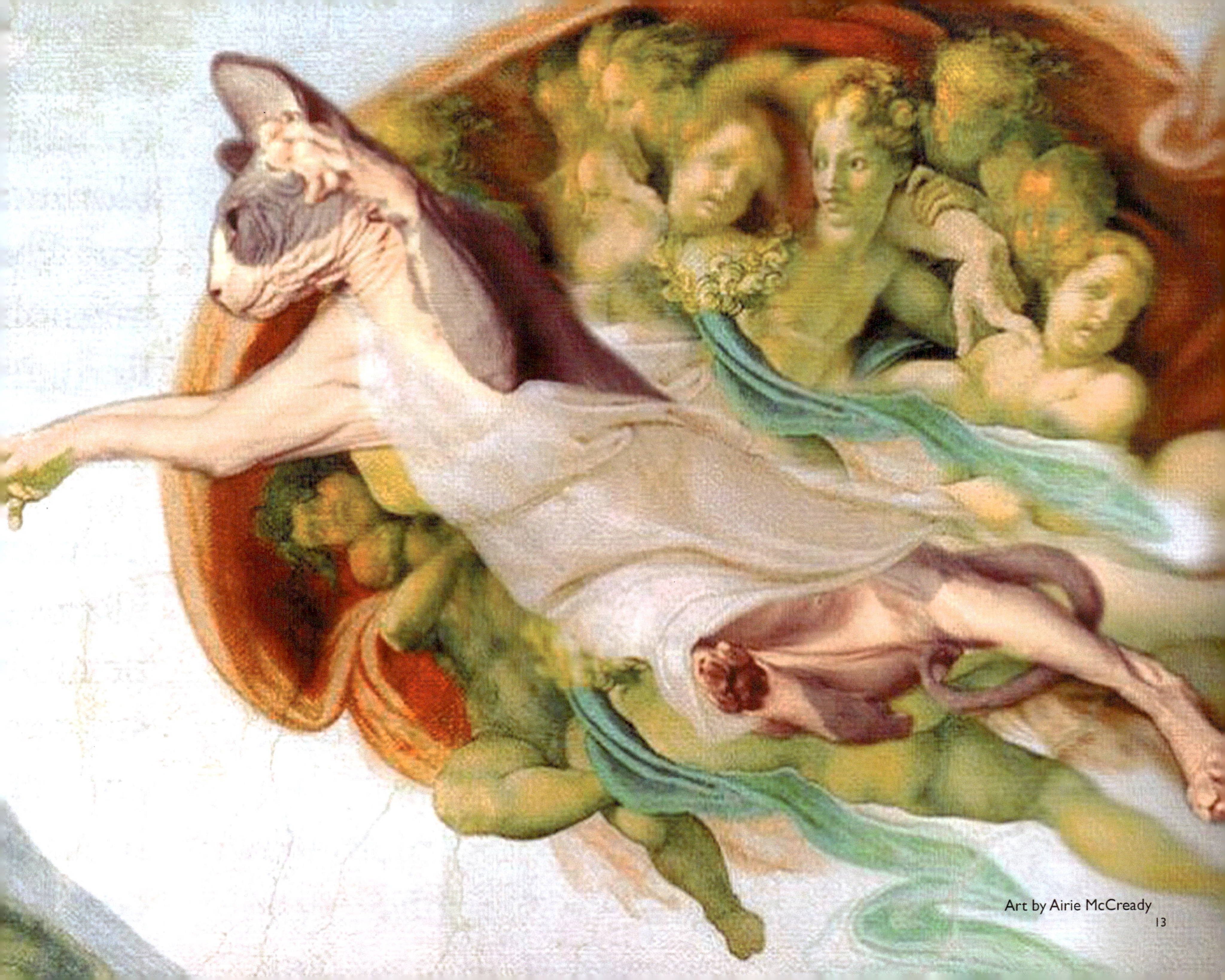
Art by Airie McCready

Twinkle

Twinkle, how you twinkle, dancing in your sleep.
Toes twitch, eyes flutter, falling, oh so deep.
Little noises, little angel he burbles and he trills,
sing song, as he dreams along and I sit oh so still.
I don't want to wake him, my little sleeping boy.
So peaceful in his blanket, dreaming of his toys.

His beauty, his birdsong, his running tippy toes.
What does my Starr Blue dream?
I wonder where he goes.
Now streching out his front legs, point hind legs toward the sky.
Beautific beaming sphynx face, It must be he can fly.

What does any cat see when their eyes are closed so tight?
I so want to dream with him, see what he sees at night.
Now an S curve, a C curve,
a shape that should not be
and he bends almost backwards, moving closer to me.

So fluid! So graceful! (But only while he sleeps!)
Now he mumbles something softly
a secret that he keeps?
I lean in to listen, perhaps now he can speak!
He awakens! Eyes open, paws pat me on my cheek.
My eyes well up and I hold him close-
for the love that we both seek.
A leg snakes up and pulls me down
he nuzzles my wet cheek.

He may not be human - but I feel not quite too-
together we are better
my one and his are more than two.
He sleeps again, against my chest,
now I am falling too...
my little love, so soft and warm,
I love you my Starr Blue!

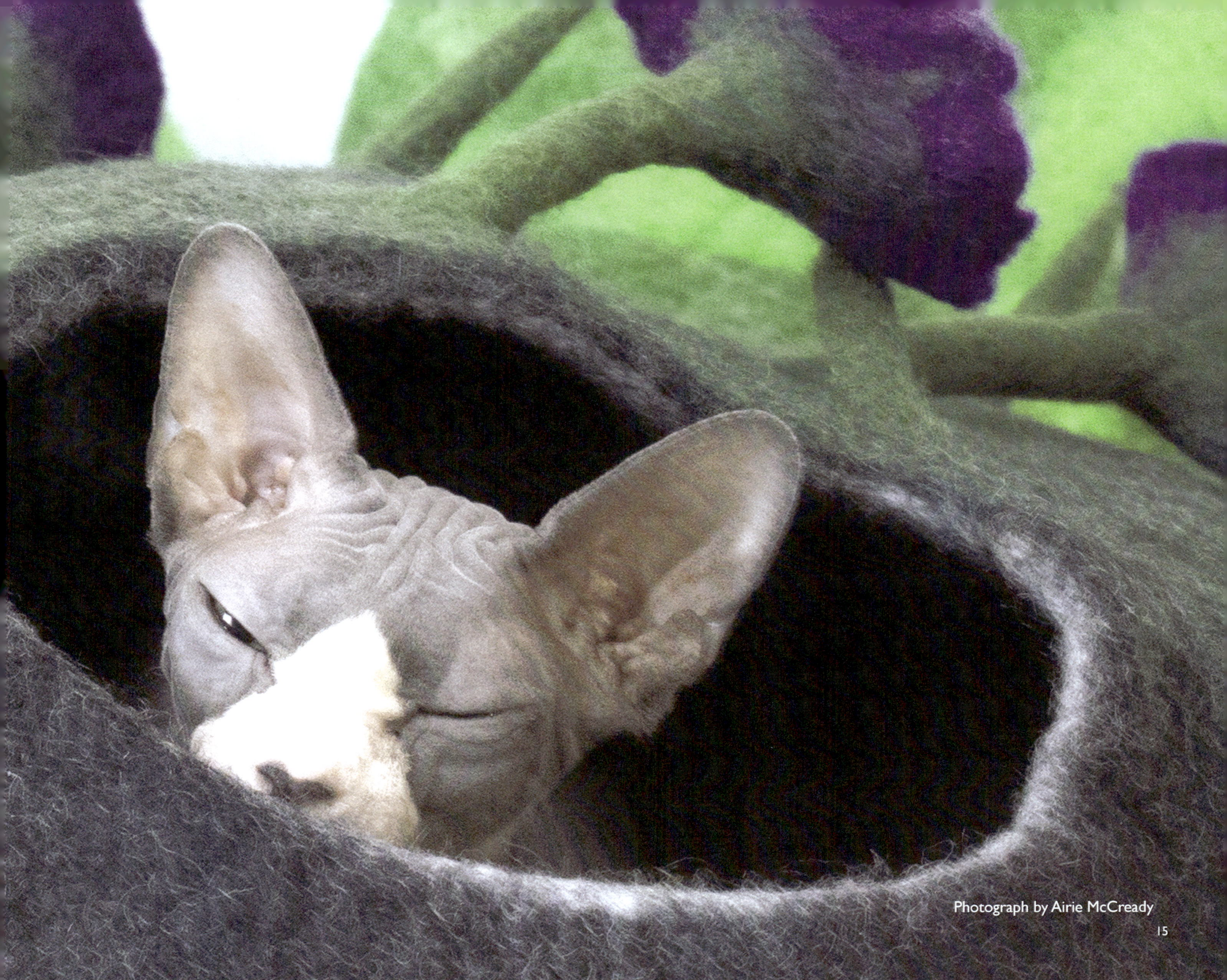

Photograph by Airie McCready

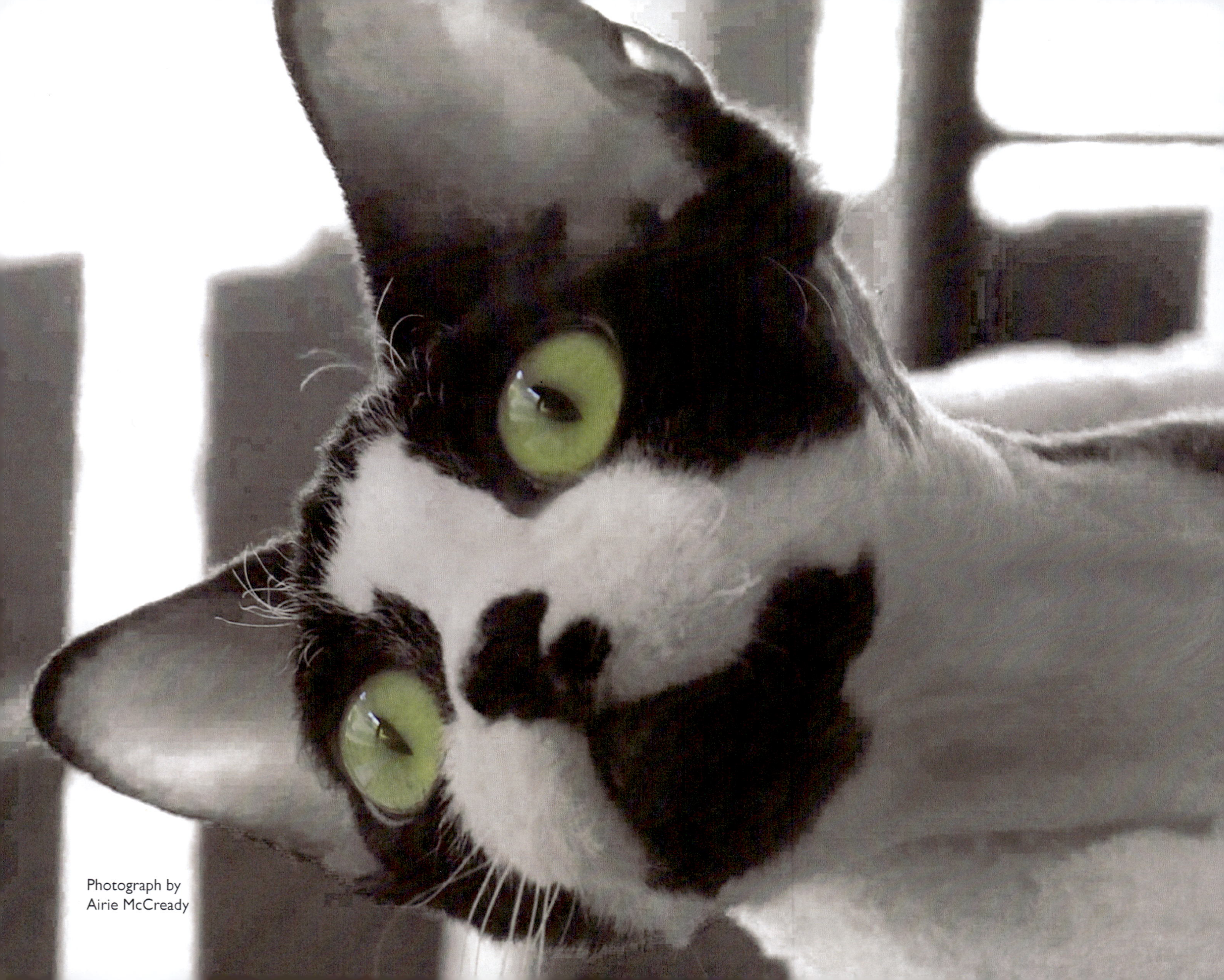
Photograph by
Airie McCready

If their souls had a song

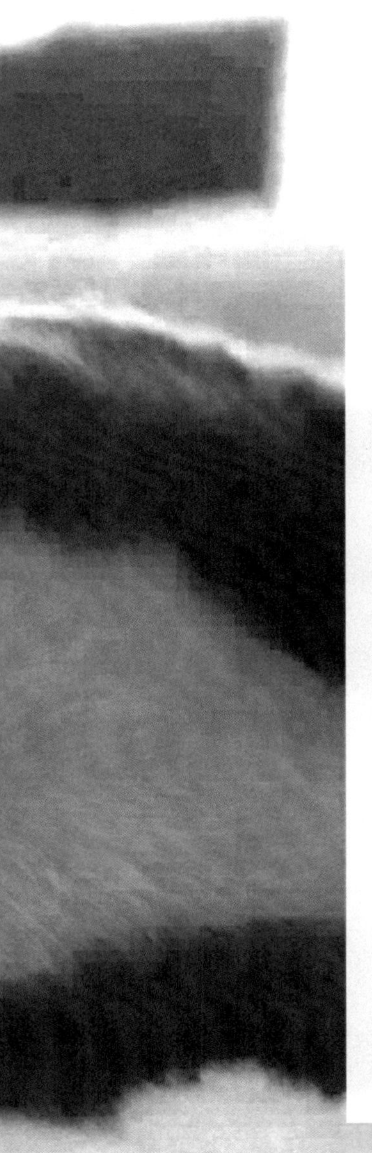

I have a camera that's inside my eye,
it goes out of focus when I laugh or I cry.
Only this camera catches all the love that I see,
My little babies are always posing for me.
Sometimes they run, and sometimes they play,
then my minds eye video stores it all away.
They cuddle or tussle or smack the other's head,
then curl up all sleepy by me in my bed.
If their sweetness had a scent it'd be warm baking bread,
if it had a design it'd be the wrinkles on their heads.
If their love had a color, it'd be one with no name,
or a deep throbbing purple with lavender flames.
If their mischief had a sound it'd be loudly chirping birds,
and dishes all breaking and laughing hard words.
If their souls had a song, I'd sing it all day,
while my minds eye camera kept snapping away.

Daisy

There are methods to my madness there are reason's for my rules.
I can be kind in spirit but I do not suffer fools.
I sit upon my throne that you refer to as your bed.
As queen upon my castle I scream "off with all your heads!"
I may be small in stature but my voice is huge and shrill.
Whether toy or treasure live I move in for the kill.
If I make a grumble there is reason to take heed -
My mood goes dark and thunderous with an unimpeded speed.
In the morning I wake slowly for I have some pain in me.
I take my nasty medicine so I can run and see.
Though the peasants eat their break-fast I will not come when I'm called.
I will not eat when they are near or watch me, not at all.
And though my eyes are tearing it is not because I cry.
I was sick when I was little and it scarred up both my eyes.
Don't touch me when I'm sleeping, only when I ask you to.
Don't pick me up but stand stock still so I may jump on you.
If I like you I will bless you with my silly Daisy dance,
Twirl upon your shoulders and then down into your lap.
I'll lick you and I'll purr and roll, and oh how you'll love me!
But don't you try to stop it or you'll hear my mighty scream!
Don't you tell a soul that I can have a heart of gold.
Or I'll turn on you and growl and screech until your blood runs cold!
I'm beautiful and soft and small and sweet and oh so dear,
And I will live forever, so please have no nightmare fears.
I'm tiny and I'm mighty and I'm quite a sight to see.
Don't piss me off or I'll show you just what it means to pee!
Unpredictable, uncontrollable, unbridled and unknown,
I am cat and I am Sphynx and I am terrible and alone.
But if the day is long and then the night is longer still,
I'll cuddle you and love you now if you are feeling ill.
I may not always come and kiss you for I'm muddled in my eyes.
Don't fear for me, and pity me, I'm much to strong to die!
There are methods to my madness, and a little crazy too -
But never for a moment doubt that I - I do love you.

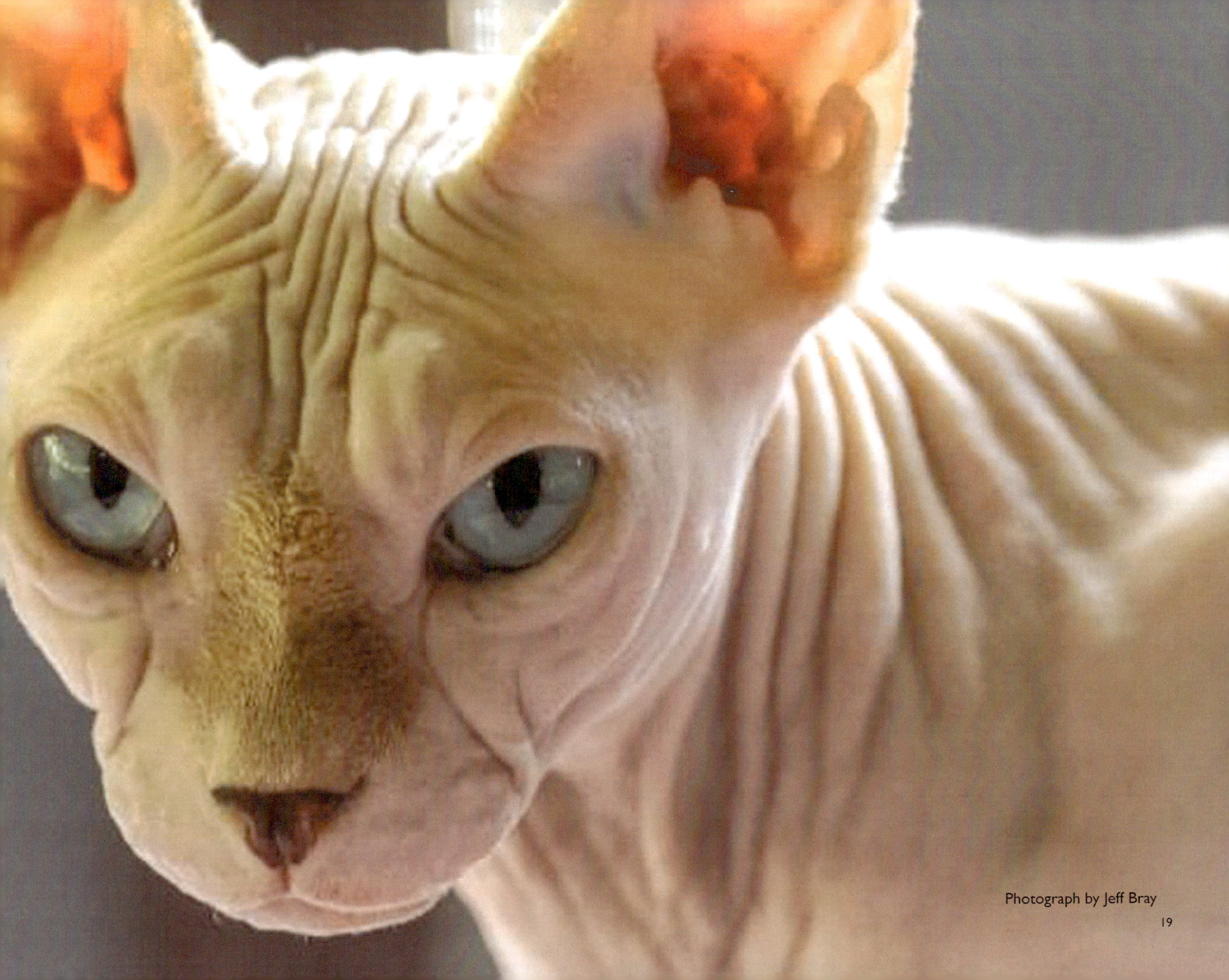

Photograph by Jeff Bray

Sealed in a Purr

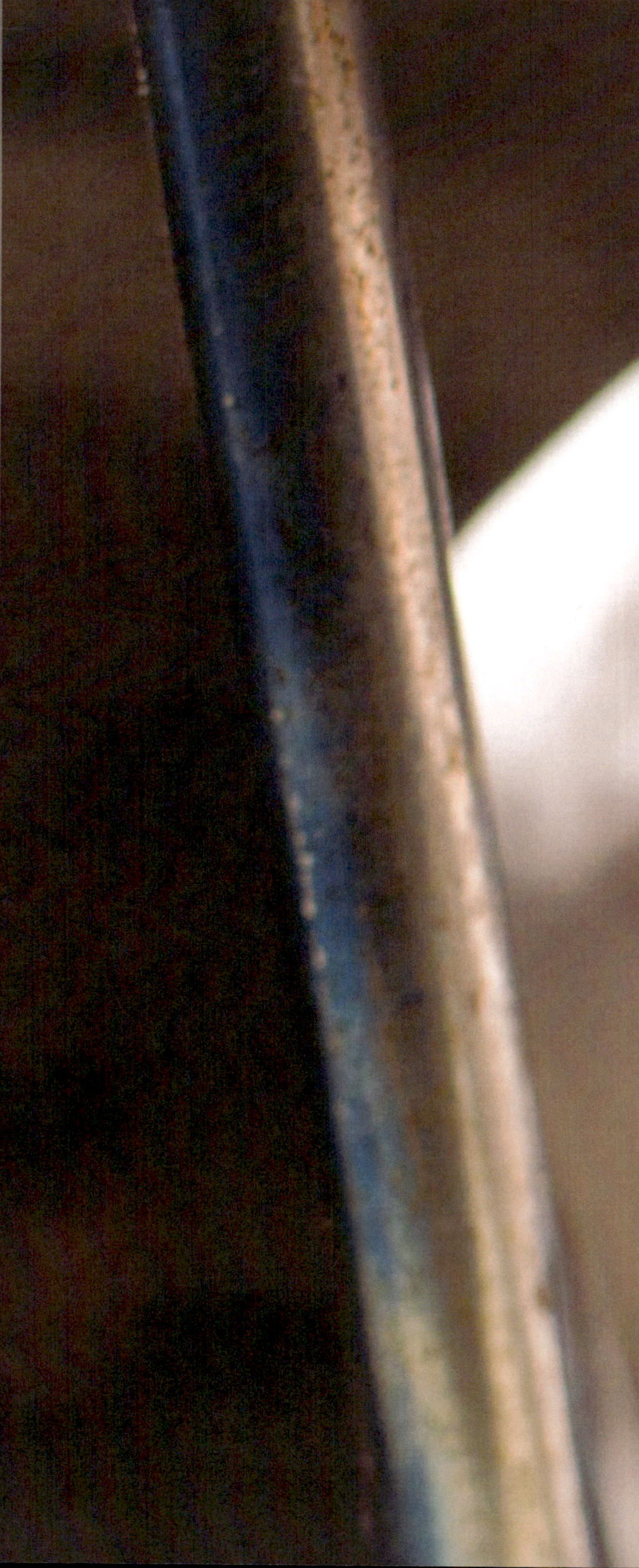

Deep not dark but bright and strong,
So little to have lived so many lives so long.
White is the outline and gold is the light,
that shone in my waking dream of him tonight.
His eyes have depths I have never seen,
Multiple colors of blue, and green.
His body is large, his heart larger still,
He possesses a positive yet tentative will.

His soul so pure it shines on high,
His soul so good I almost cry,
A soul born to earth for many times,
A soul that is perfectly sublime.

Deep not dark so white and pure,
In his eyes lives our world's one perfect cure.
If only they would stop-
If only all could see-
The love that could heal-
And how it could be.

All of the living all have souls.
And until we can see, none can be whole.
Deep.
Not Dark.
So White.
So Pure.
Enclosed in a kitten.
Sealed with a purr.

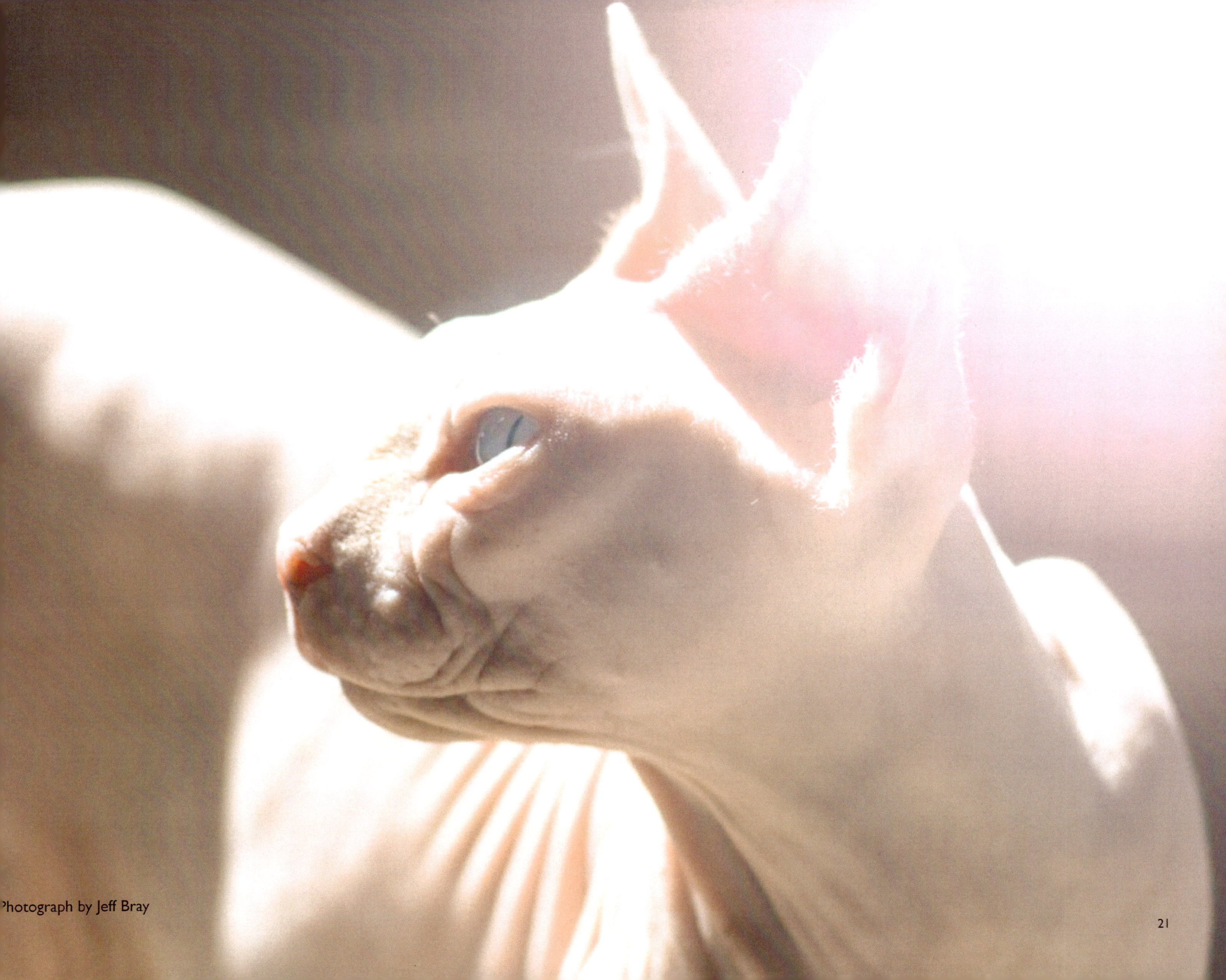

Starry Sky

We lay in bed, my cats and I,
the bedroom ceiling a starry sky.
The crumpled sheets and blankets too
wrap us in a nest that says I love you.
We sleep entwined, my cats and me
in a dreamy river and a salty sea

I love their warmth, and crave their skin
The velvet softness where their noses begin.
Their heat though, it can sometimes be
a roasting flame that tortures me.

We look through the windows, my cats and I,
at the little birds nesting and the clear blue sky.
We can't go out under the sun,
their skin as sensitive as mine's become.
But in the shade and filtered light,
we can love the day as we love the night.

We are scary ghouls, my cats and me,
pale and soft and glowing to see.
Some are frightened at very first sight,
But we don't care, we have the night.

All true beauty lays in the heart,
If you can't see that, you're not so smart.
A hairless cat, a tattoo'd girl,
are the most beautiful things in the whole wide world.

We lay in bed, my cats and I
Our love as big as the starry sky.

Art by Airie McCready

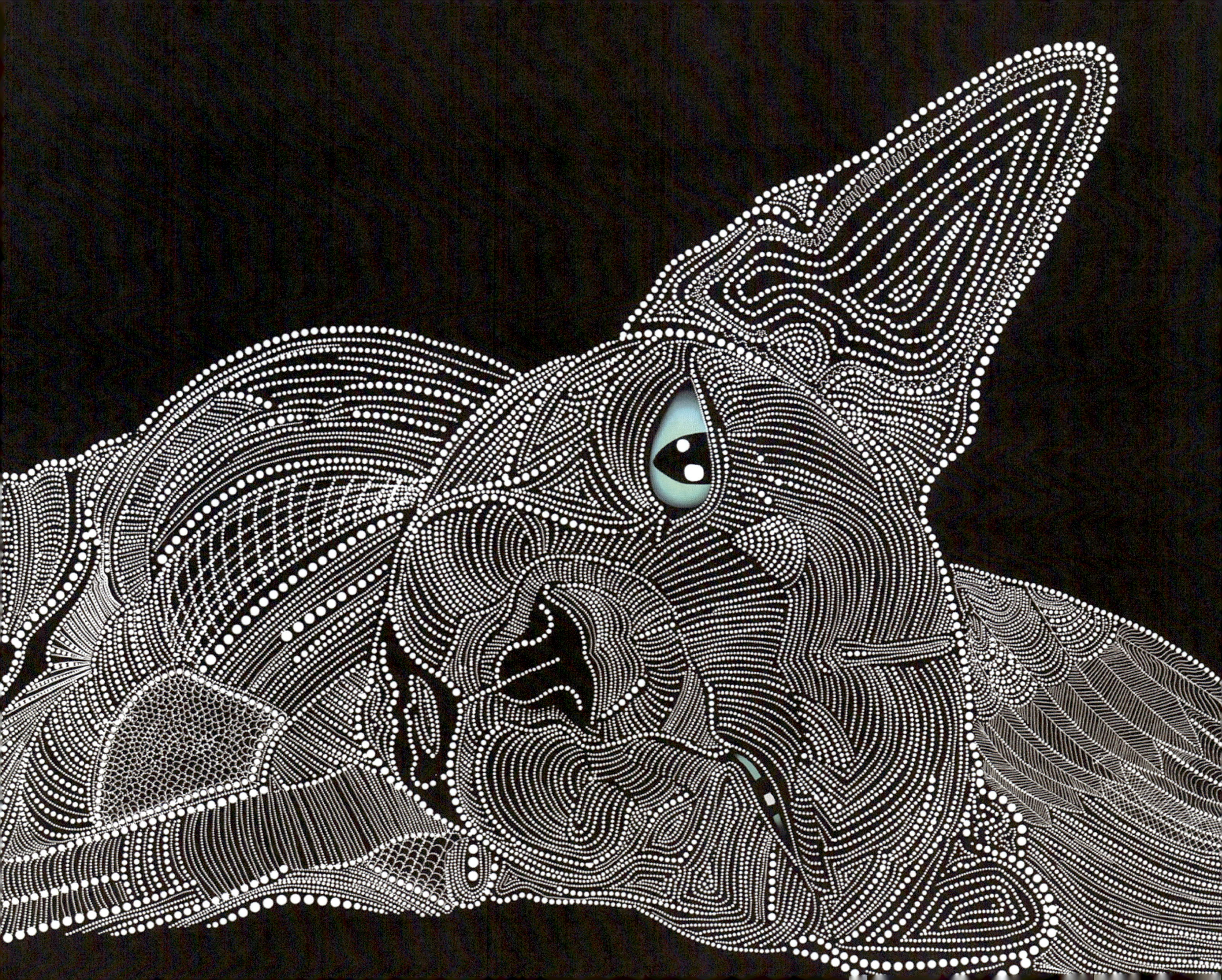

Lucky

The walls are filled with whispers,
My eyes they fill with tears.
I miss the scent of your sweet head,
And want to hold you near.

His soft face held between my hands
As I whispered my goodbye,
I said, "I'll make the bad stop now,"
To my giant, gentle boy.

And as his gold eyes slowly dimmed,
And the pain it washed away,
The fear was gone but so was he
Up to heaven so he could play.

The kindest way was cruel to me,
His face it haunts me still,
But I'm glad I was there,
and that I could help,
but now I feel chilled.

So I think of him at a flat out run,
His breathing so easy and deep
As he leaps and catches dragonflies-
That's always mine to keep.

And the ocean of love that crashed down on me,
it almost makes it okay-
the love for my big Lucky Boy
Will last forever and a day.

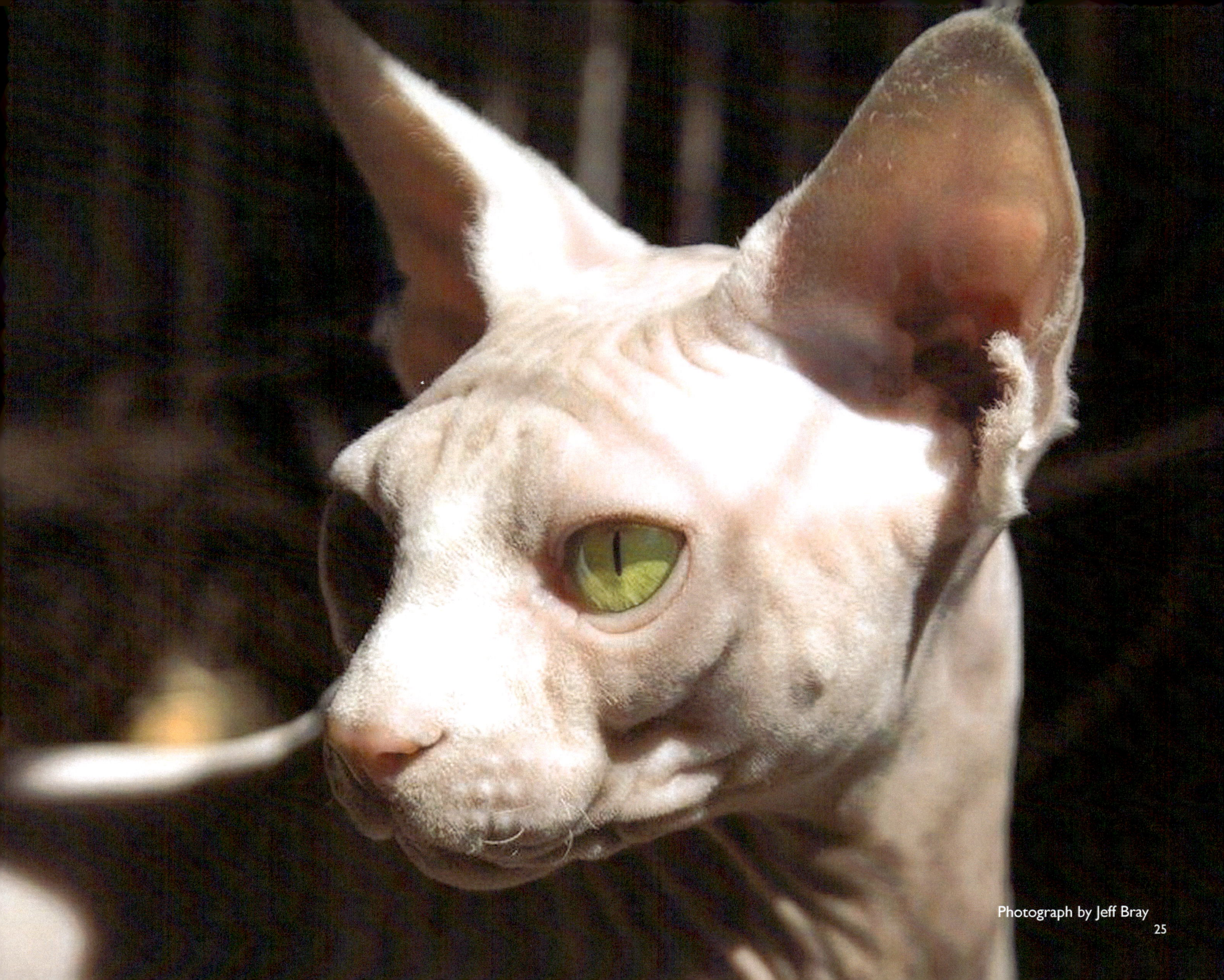

Photograph by Jeff Bray

Now I Chase the Stars

In a dream, I watch him at play,
running up to the door, then dashing away.
His nose is so rosy, his eyes are so clear,
no catch to the breathing of my Lucky dear.

His eyes glow like lanterns, first green and then gold,
He stands in the doorway, the question so old-
In or out my dear kitty? As many asked before,
Because you know that a cat loves to stand by the door.

He sets one paw in, then draws it back,
I close the door down to not even a crack,
then BOOM! how he hits it and comes bursting in!
and if a cat could smile, well they can, and he grins!

And again, and again, and again Lucky boy,
and he leaps, and he spins, through the door with his toys.
But as the light fades in the grey winter sky,
He turns to me and he meows, and he says good-bye.

Then he speaks in our words, "Mom please don't you cry,
all of us go, to live in the sky.
I just went to soon, I just went too fast,
I wish I could have warned you what would come to pass."

"So think of me with love when you open the door,
and when the wind blows like I liked from before,
with the leaves all a swirling, how I chased them so free,
Now I chase stars, and the stars play with me."

RIP my Lucky, with the softest nose in the world, I will never, ever forget you.

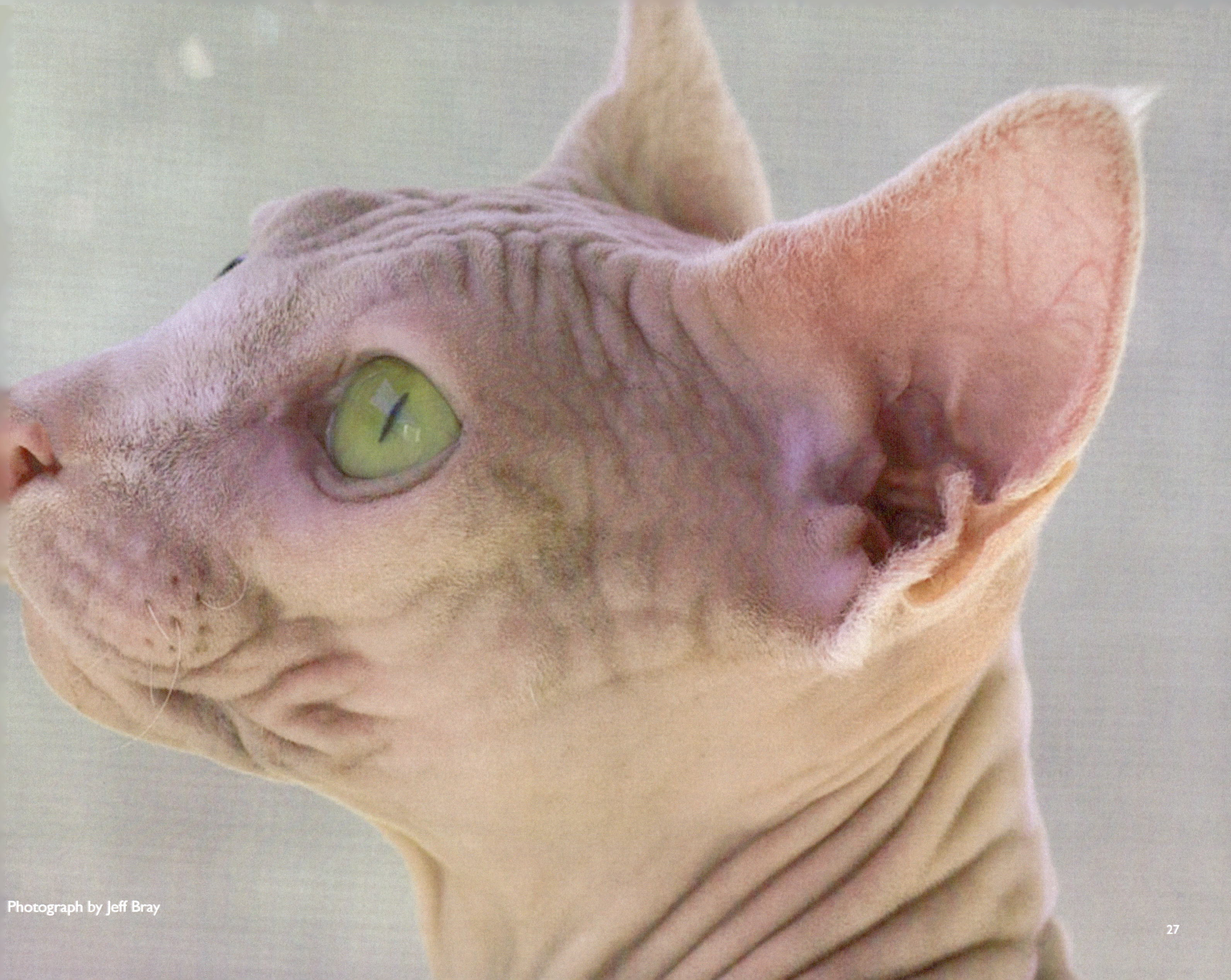

Devlin

The house was much quieter before you arrived,
There wasn't a day when I hadn't cried.
You were quickly brought to me, and I was afraid-
What would be the results of a choice quickly made?
As we drove up to get you I was anxious and stressed-
what if you didn't like me, or like to get dressed?
If you were not a model kitty, that was fine with me,
But if you didn't like me? Who could forsee?
You were tiny and curly with a very loud MIAOW
When set loose in the room, you were sweet, and how,
Could I ever have doubted you'd be my new love,
Sent to me by my Lucky who'd gone far above.
Your hummingbird purr, your sweet blinking eyes,
You smiled at me, and there was no disguise,
I almost teared up but you capered away,-and I laughed!
For the first time out loud since "that day."
You came home and went straight to work on my heart,
Did you know what was coming? How you would play a part?
For your sneezing took us to the doctors that day,
And with you I noticed Starr was tired when he played.
And when the news came that Starr's heart was broken too-
You comforted me when the tears came anew.
You patted my face with your soft little touch,
Thank goodness you were here-I needed you much!
The house is much brighter now that you arrived,
And it is very seldom that I really cry.
I'm braced for the future with much less dismay-
Though my Lucky is gone, my luck, it has stayed.

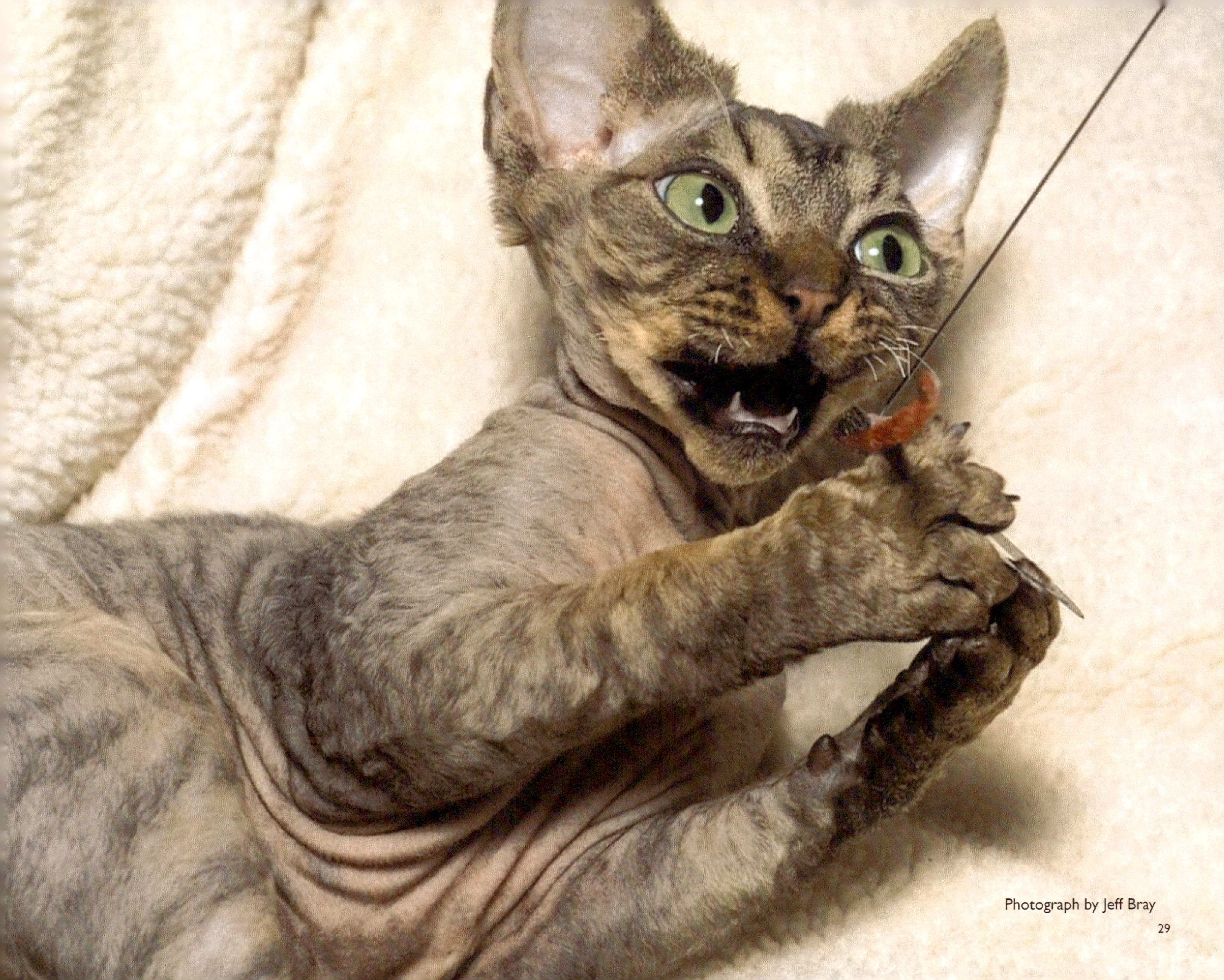

Photograph by Jeff Bray

Curly Thing

Nah, my little curly thing,
sleepy, meows with a raucous ring.
Tiny but strong, naked but furred
dislike the method by which we occurred.
Love you so much though it's only three days,
Bright eyes and wedge'd head and smile as you lay
Curled in my arms, or right by my side,
If I said you were the same, then I might have lied.
Little Devlin, my Devon, my son and new cat,
How your big brother loves you and how I love that.
Though the sisters are hissers, they will love you too,
One day they will groom you, the cream and the blue.
The softness, how funny your little furred brow,
Swore never a furred one, but I know now,
you were meant to be here to heal my heart,
'Tis Lucky who did this so we'd never part.
Little naked but furred one, fuzzy curly thing,
you and I are together for what the future may bring.
How I love you as you run with your puffed little tail,
when you leap and you caper, I feel my heart sail.
Goodnight Devlin, my Devon, my heart healing cat.
Though time it will take, it really can do that.
Little purr love, little pure love, so different so new,
Ah, my little Devon, how I love you!

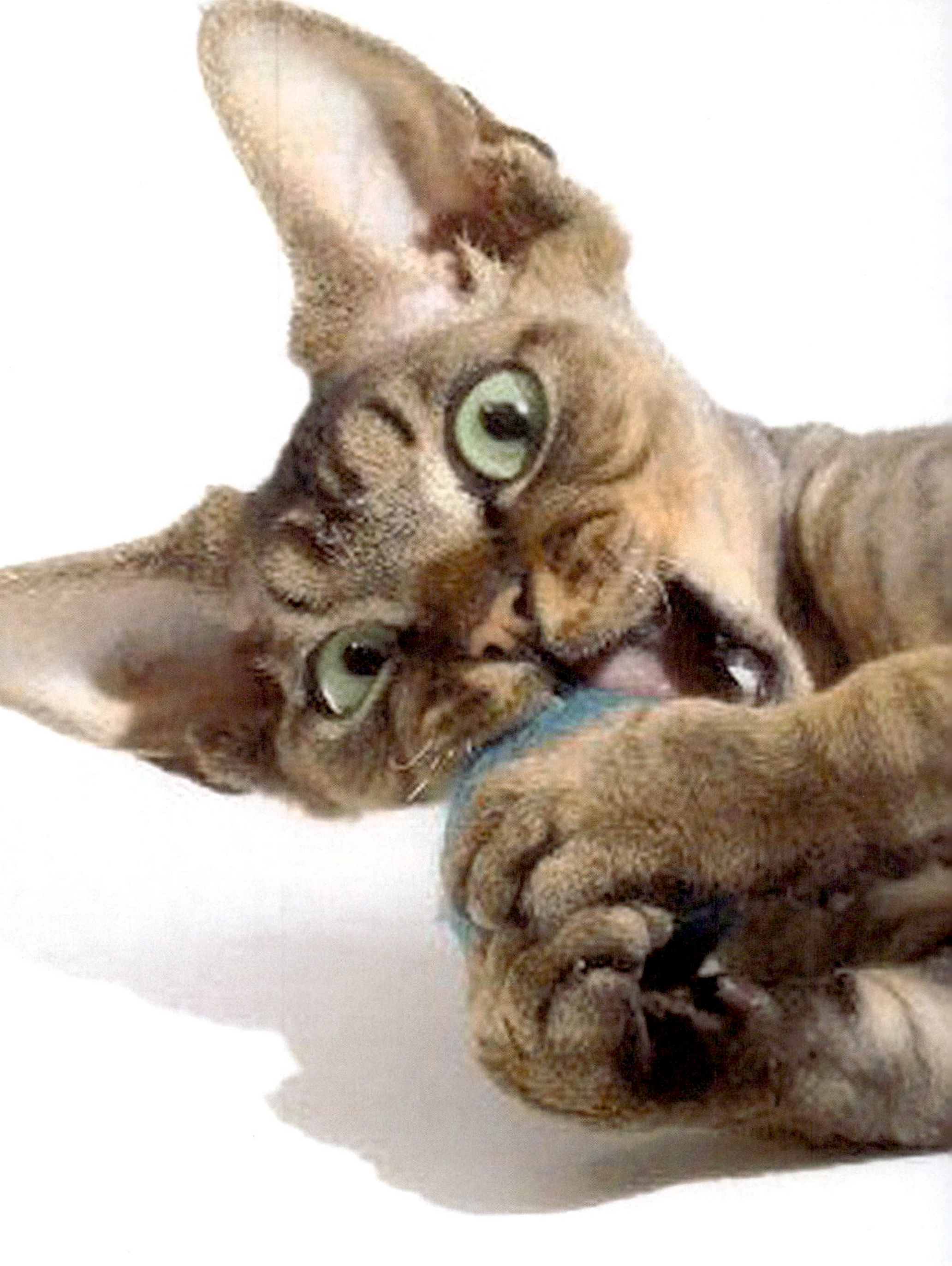

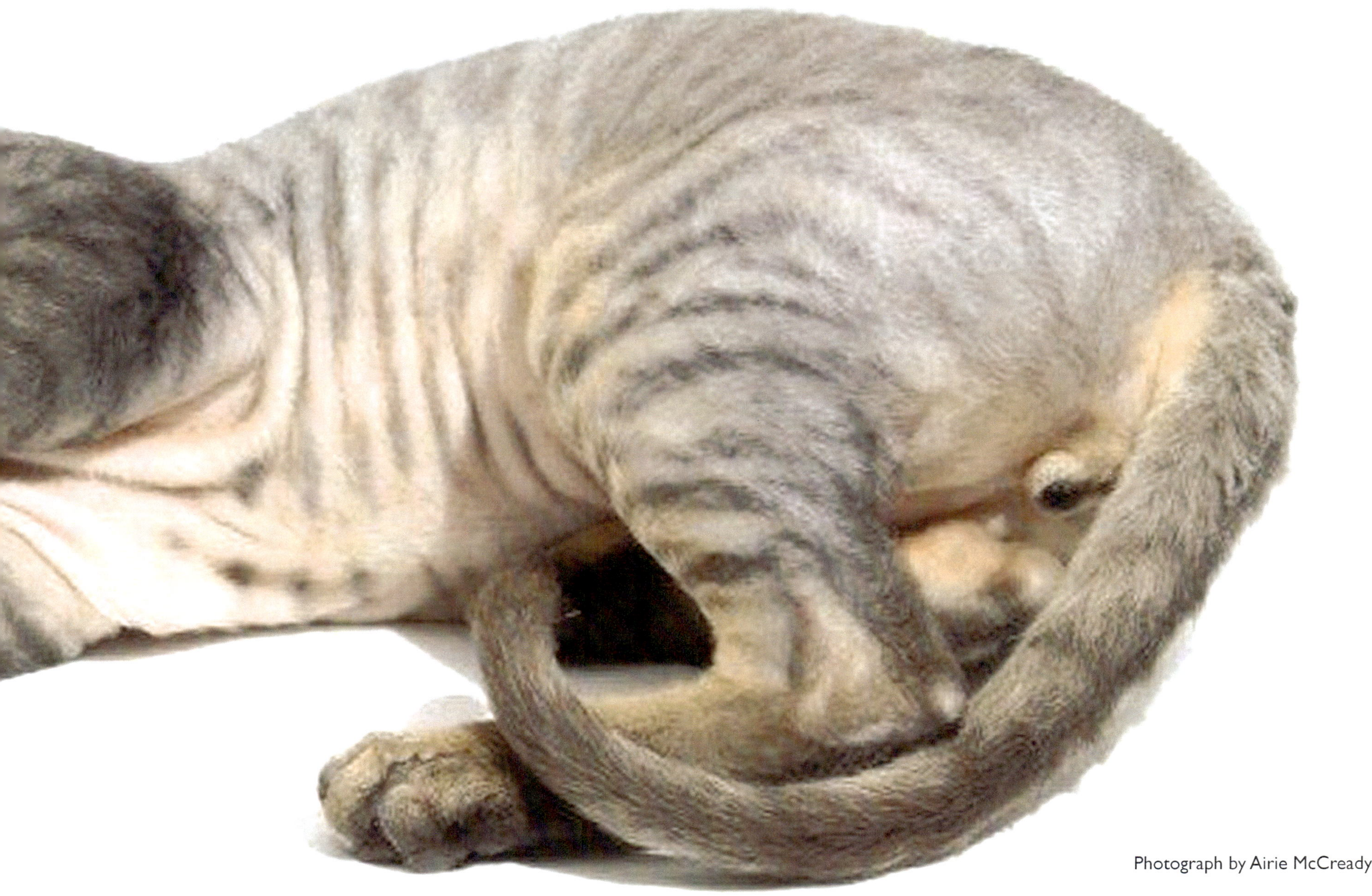

Photograph by Airie McCready

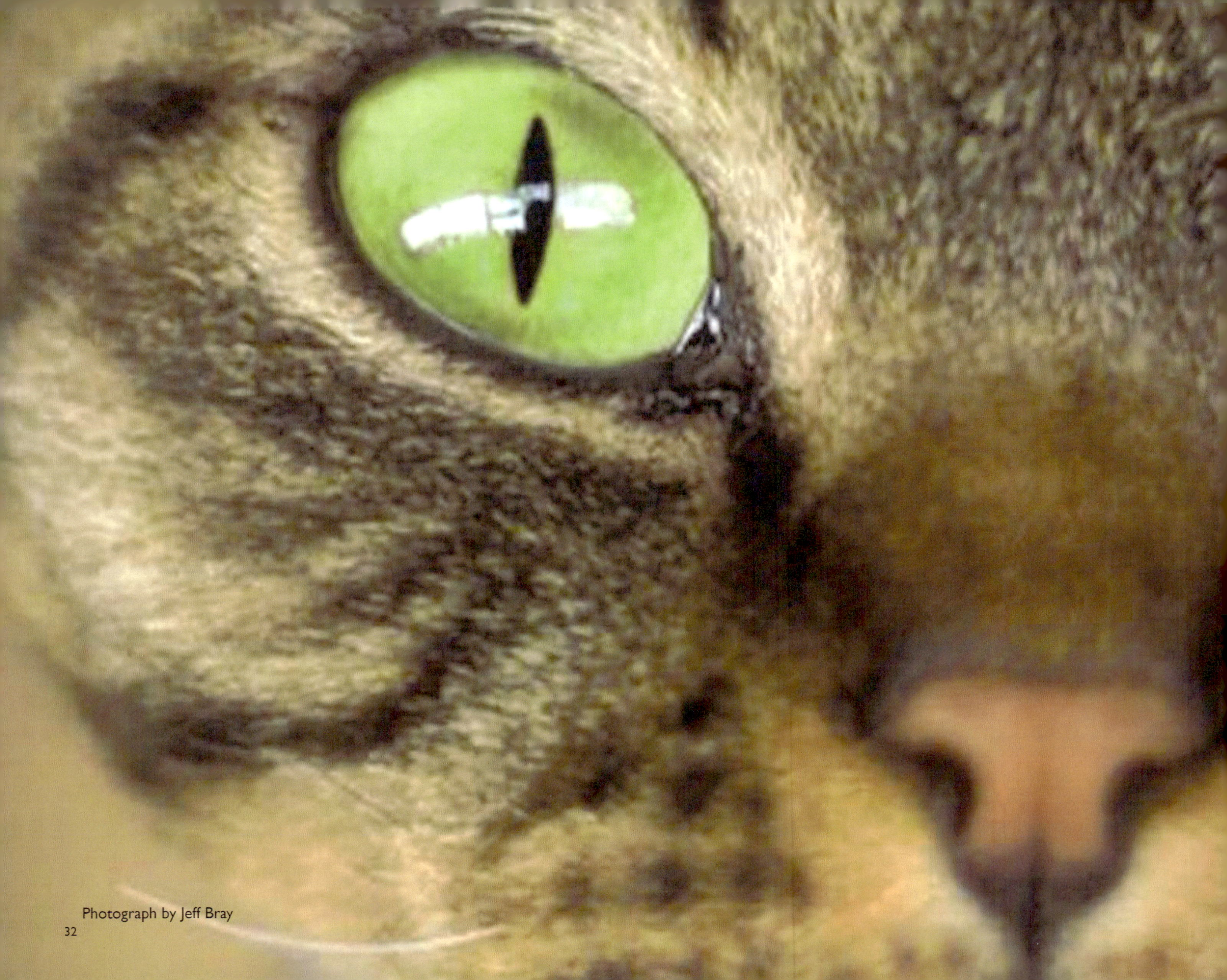

Photograph by Jeff Bray

A Clock & A Cat

What is it in that tempered gaze,
of green and gold upon my face
that helps my heart to heal anew,
every time I think of you.

That tiny body close to mine,
earthbound creature yet divine,
an angels gaze, a mother's touch
such a small paw to hold so much.

And as you pat upon my face,
gently where the tears have traced,
I hear a voice saying oh so low,
love cannot die it can only grow.

And while it hurts and pains by day,
time will heal or at least they say.
time will heal, and a kitten too,
I wish a clock and a cat for all of you.

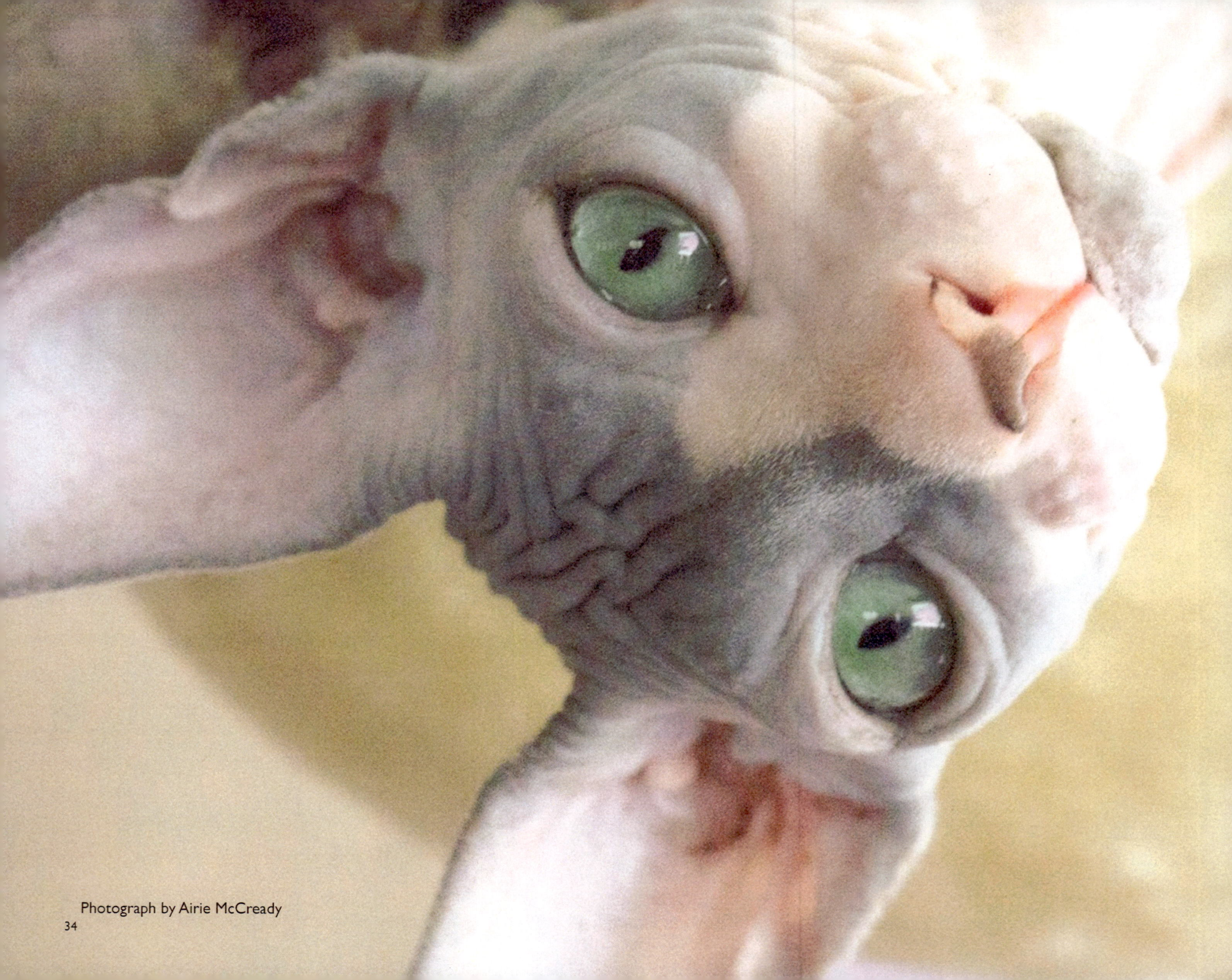

Photograph by Airie McCready

34

"I Do"

Gentle little man, with eyes of jade,
Tender little soul, so beautifully made.
Tiny dagger teeth, pressed only so much,
Sharpest little claws, but the lightest of touch.
Perfect little ears, flower petal soft,
Tiny little wrinkles, so carefully wrought.
Roundest little tum, so clean and so pink,
Tiny little tongue to take tiny long drinks.
Focus on the eyes, as the head comes up,
Roman nose doubles out, and now he looks tough.
Profile of a nobleman, a lion and a lamb,
Waddles after me, wants to know where I am.
Voice so high pitched, forming important sounds,
runs up his tree and rolls all the way down.
Wraps his arms around brother, cuddles close to my side.
Never is he arrogant, though he has pride.
Unbalanced and perfect and awkward and new,
love, your name is kitten, and I say, "I do."

One True North

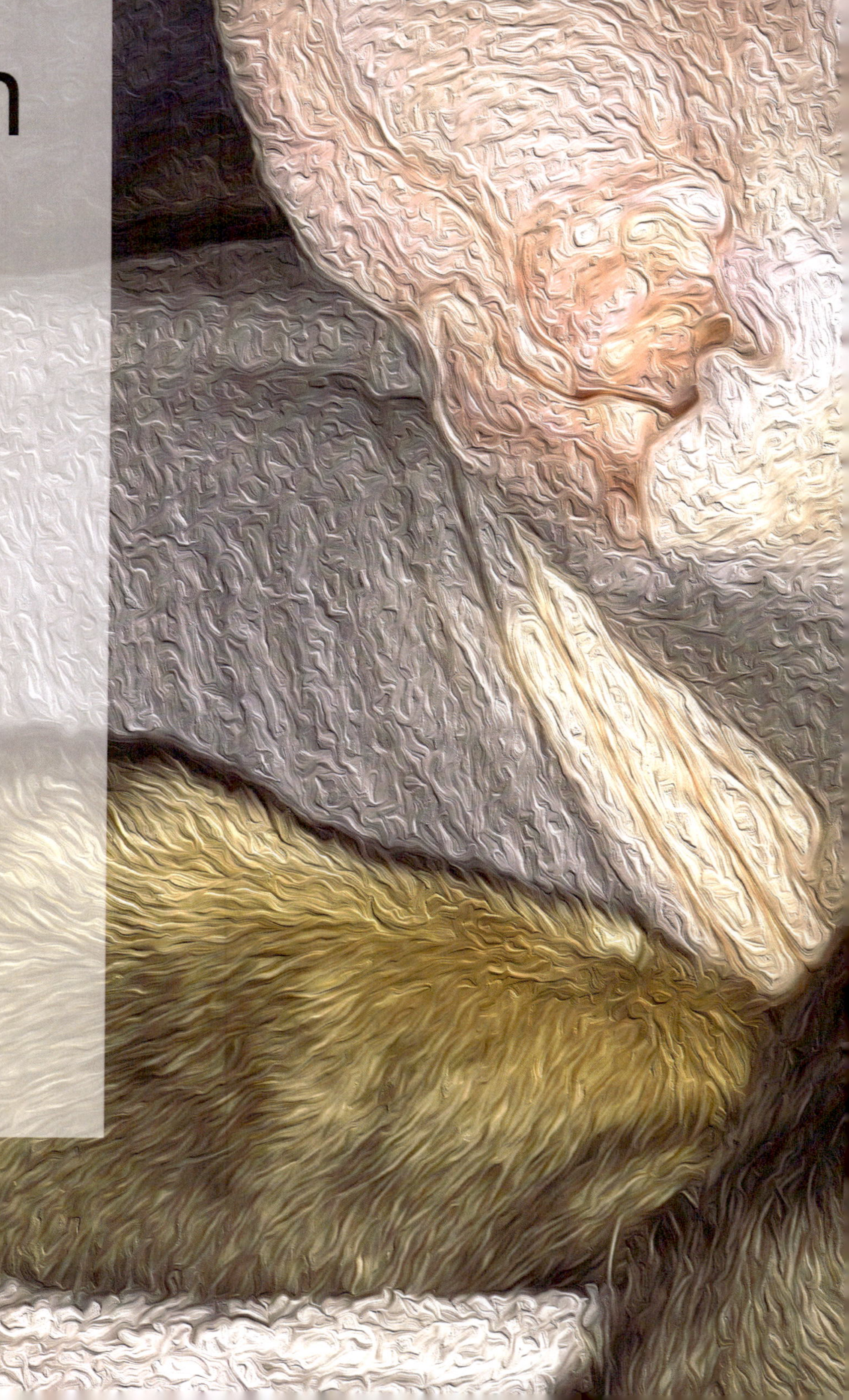

When two can love not seen aligned
For in this world a pair combined,
Nature will bless what man can't see,
the purest love of him for thee.
When gender's dismissed, and looks are too,
they allow the bind of him to you.
When age's ignored, and race and creed,
There comes a love of a different breed.
Now species stays, Nature holds that clear,
no wolf to cat, no horse to deer.
The strongest male can mother well,
The weakest female can wreak hell.
From creation comes a destructive force,
Only tempered when we find our own true North.
So let them love, it hurts no faith,
It only hurts the ones who hate.
The poison of pain, of ignorance held,
Damns them to forever live in hell.
One smile, one tear, one word of love,
Can release a heart, it is enough.
From hate can come a healing force,
Held true, hold course, to one true North.

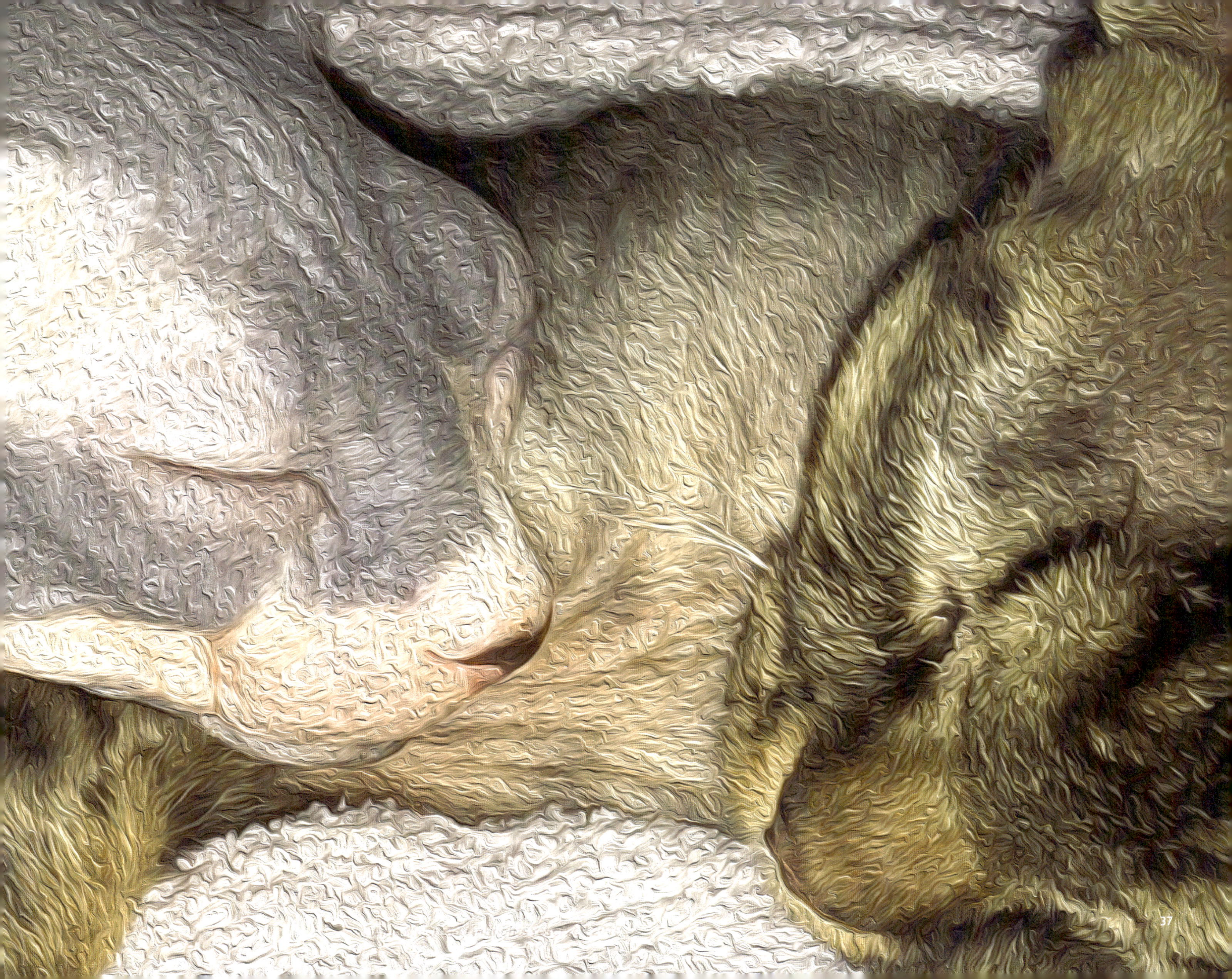

37

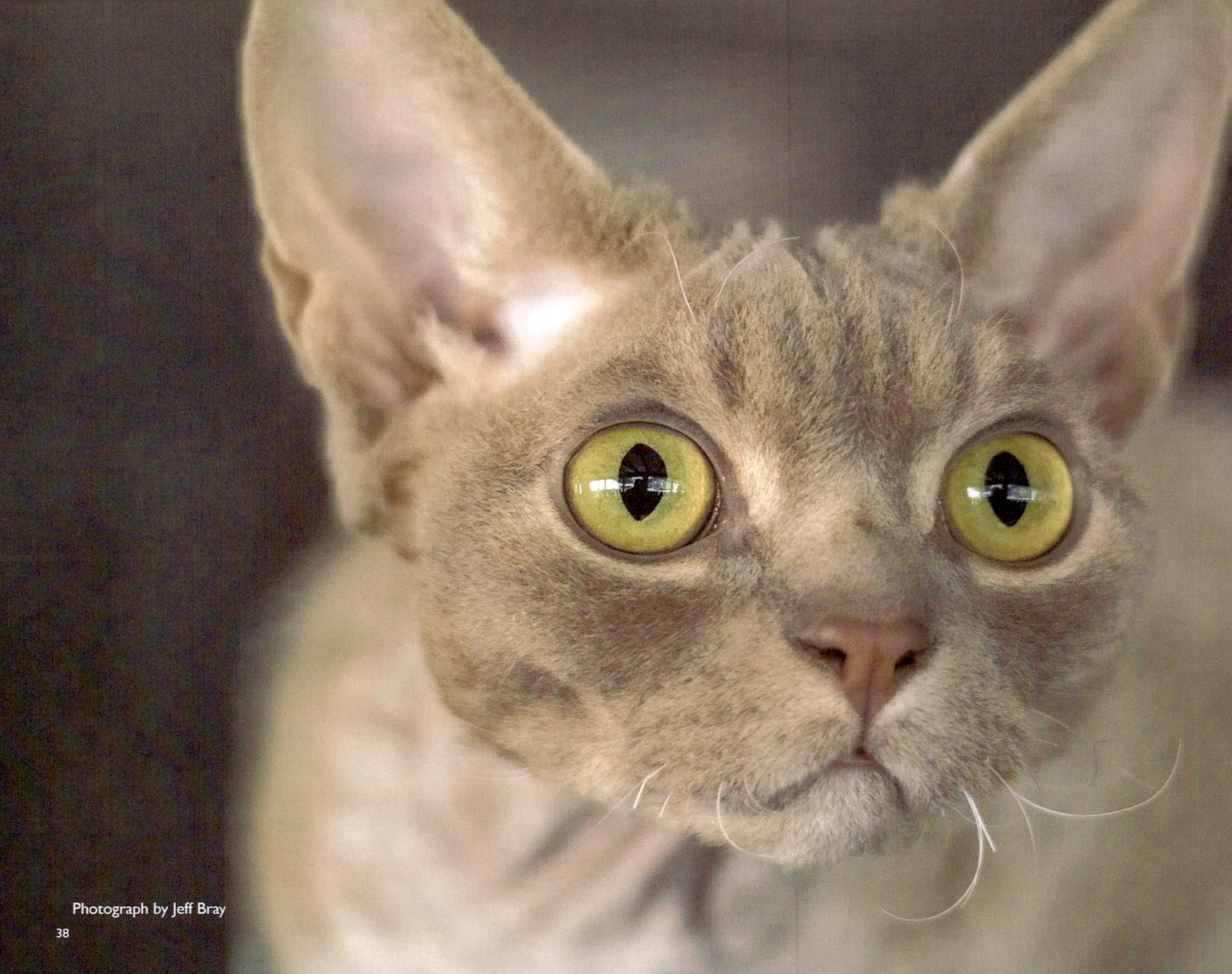
Photograph by Jeff Bray

The light that is my Rhys

My Starr he shot to heaven and
I thought the sadness would not end
I almost went to meet him there,
because you see I took no care.
Then darkness fell with sweet distaste,
All goals acheived but with much waste,
of health and energy, love and friends,
It seemed to all come to an end.
This fact of body, fright of mind,
to leave my old life far behind,
To step up and live in the light
now walk forward with no fright.
The one that was chosen weeks ago,
is here and I wonder how do they know,
That this ray of sun in the shape of a cat
Can clear the slate and erase all that.
Oh little cub, my ray of sun,
silver and gold wrapped up in one
Precious bundle with the dancing tail
Only love can now prevail.
He's with us on this journey now
He lives in the moment and can teach me how.
Such human eyes in a kitten's face,
Five felines move me with such Grace.
Smooth and skin bare rippled fur,
Spirit pawprints track where the others were,
I'm one of them and they are me,
As we welcome the light that is my Rhys.

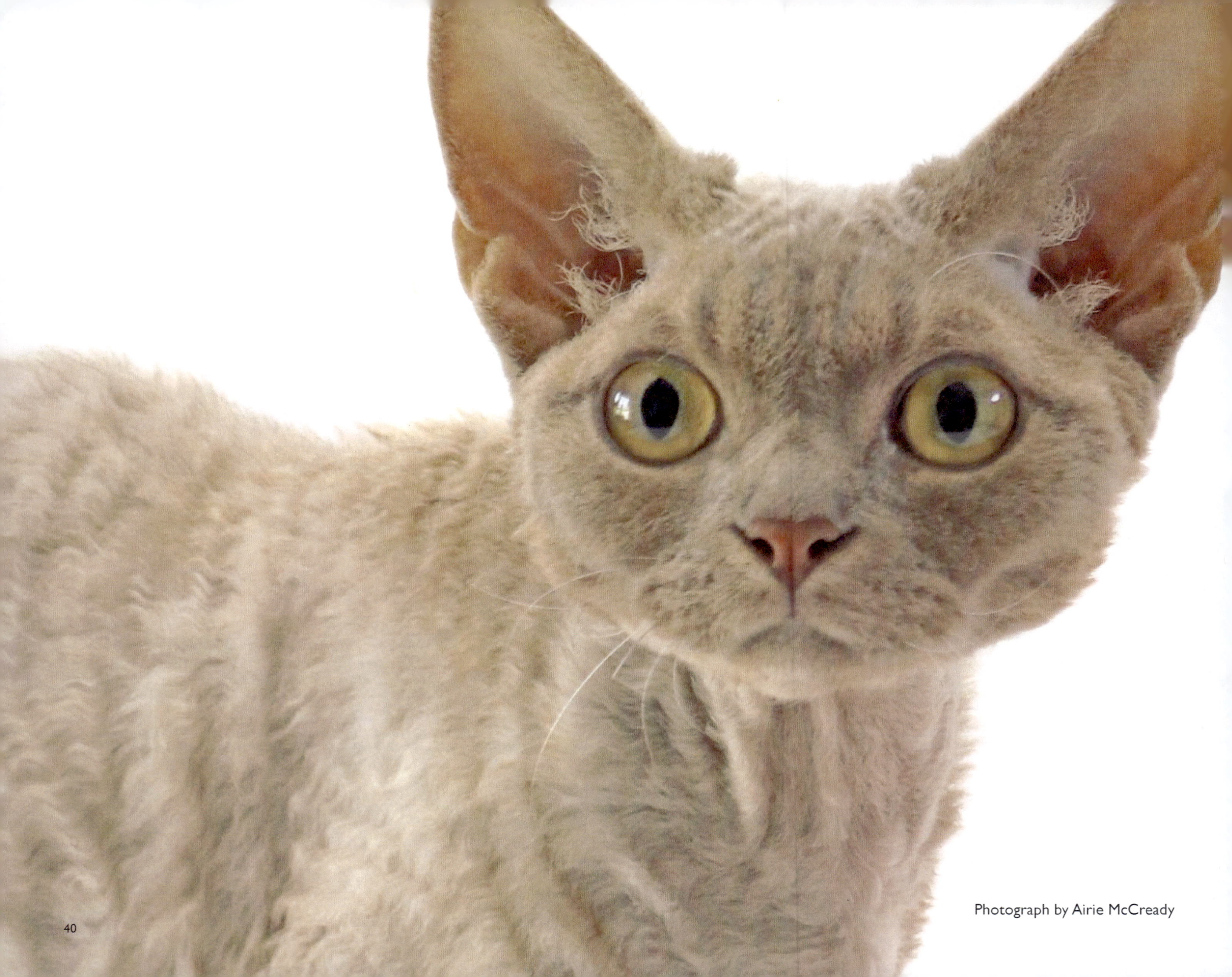

Photograph by Airie McCready

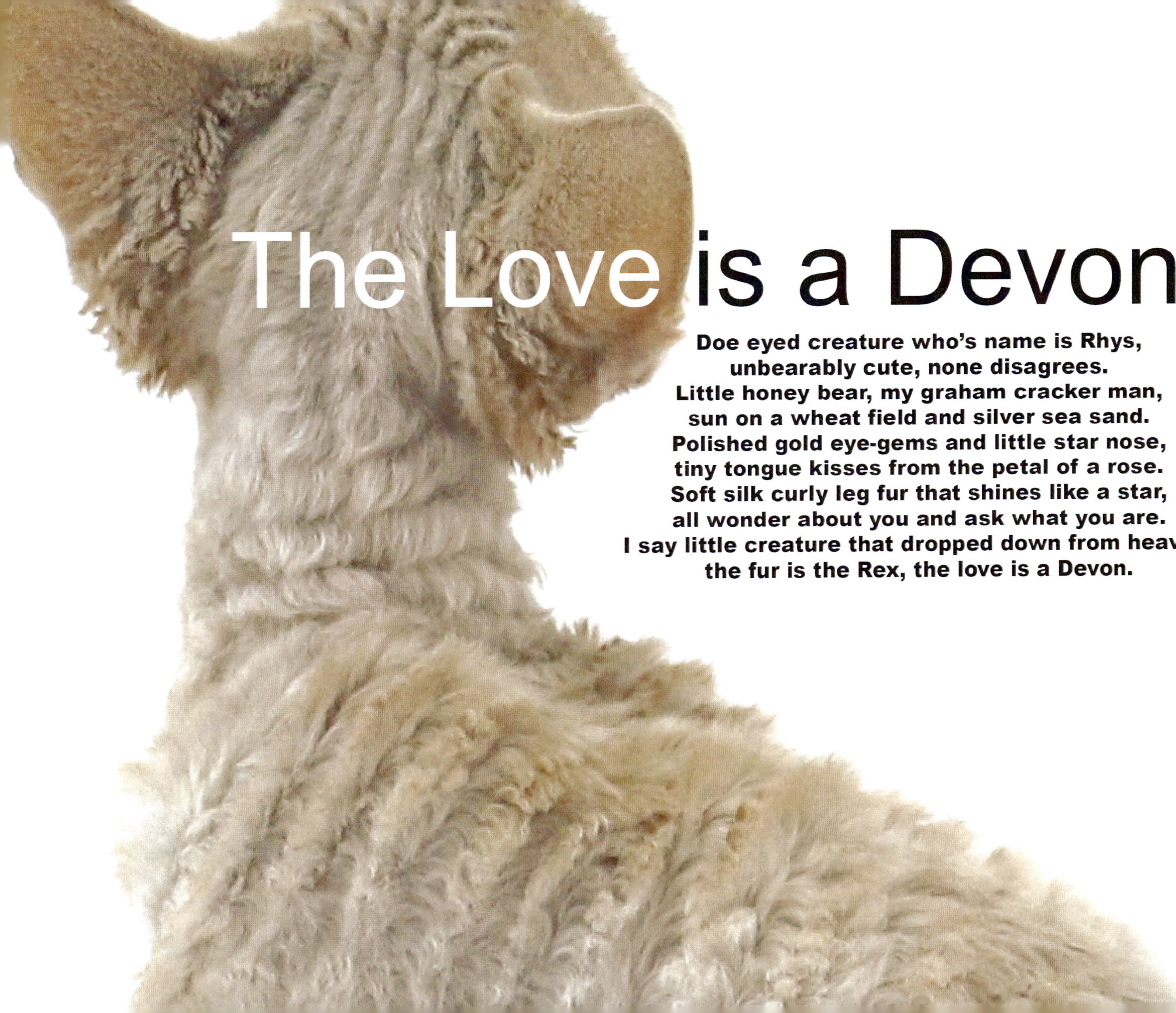

The Love is a Devon

Doe eyed creature who's name is Rhys,
unbearably cute, none disagrees.
Little honey bear, my graham cracker man,
sun on a wheat field and silver sea sand.
Polished gold eye-gems and little star nose,
tiny tongue kisses from the petal of a rose.
Soft silk curly leg fur that shines like a star,
all wonder about you and ask what you are.
I say little creature that dropped down from heaven,
the fur is the Rex, the love is a Devon.

Fever

Silent you lay in a haze of heat.
Oh how I wish that you could speak!
Tiny body it feels like you're aflame
Please give this fear a curable name.

Little eyes, one now half swollen shut.
I knew you were tired, not so sick but
Please know now that I've seen your pain
I'll do anything for you to not have it again.

Now your fever's gone but not my fear,
Are you getting better? And now there's tears,
Could I have known sooner?
What could I have done?
You are so precious my little one.

Please eat more food, and purr and tread.
In your little tent upon my bed.
Was this my fault? They all say no,
But somewhere of course, I think it's so.

I'm tethered to you by the pull of my heart,
I never want us to be apart.
Let this just be done, a chapter past,
This fearful night, let it be the last.

The sun's not yet up, but I wake and check,
Put two fingers against your neck.
You feel just warm, and thank God not
That raging fire that felt too hot.

So I slip back to sleep, and try to ignore
The thoughts of all cats that came before,
And though I'm not one who will often pray,
I quietly ask God to let you stay.

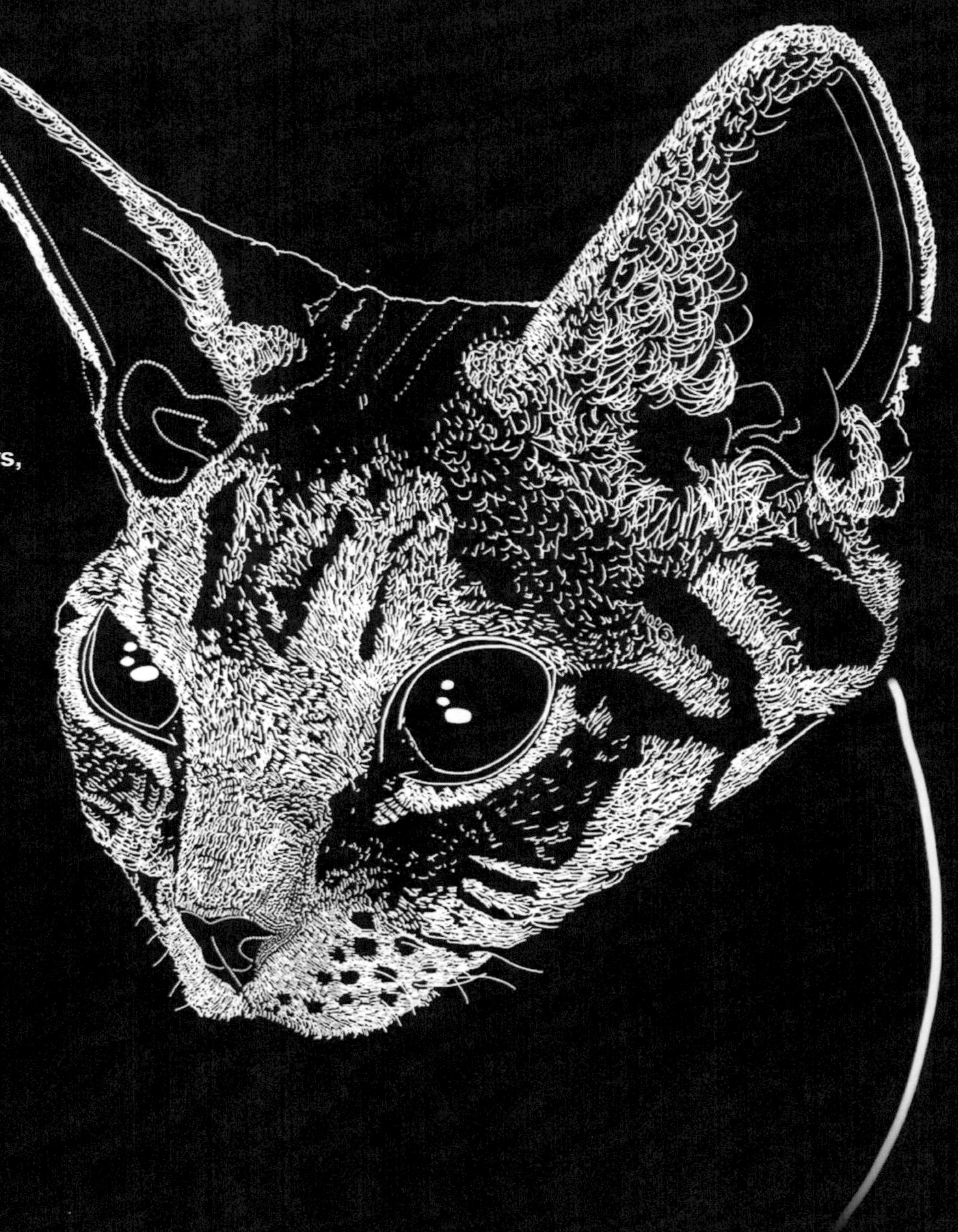

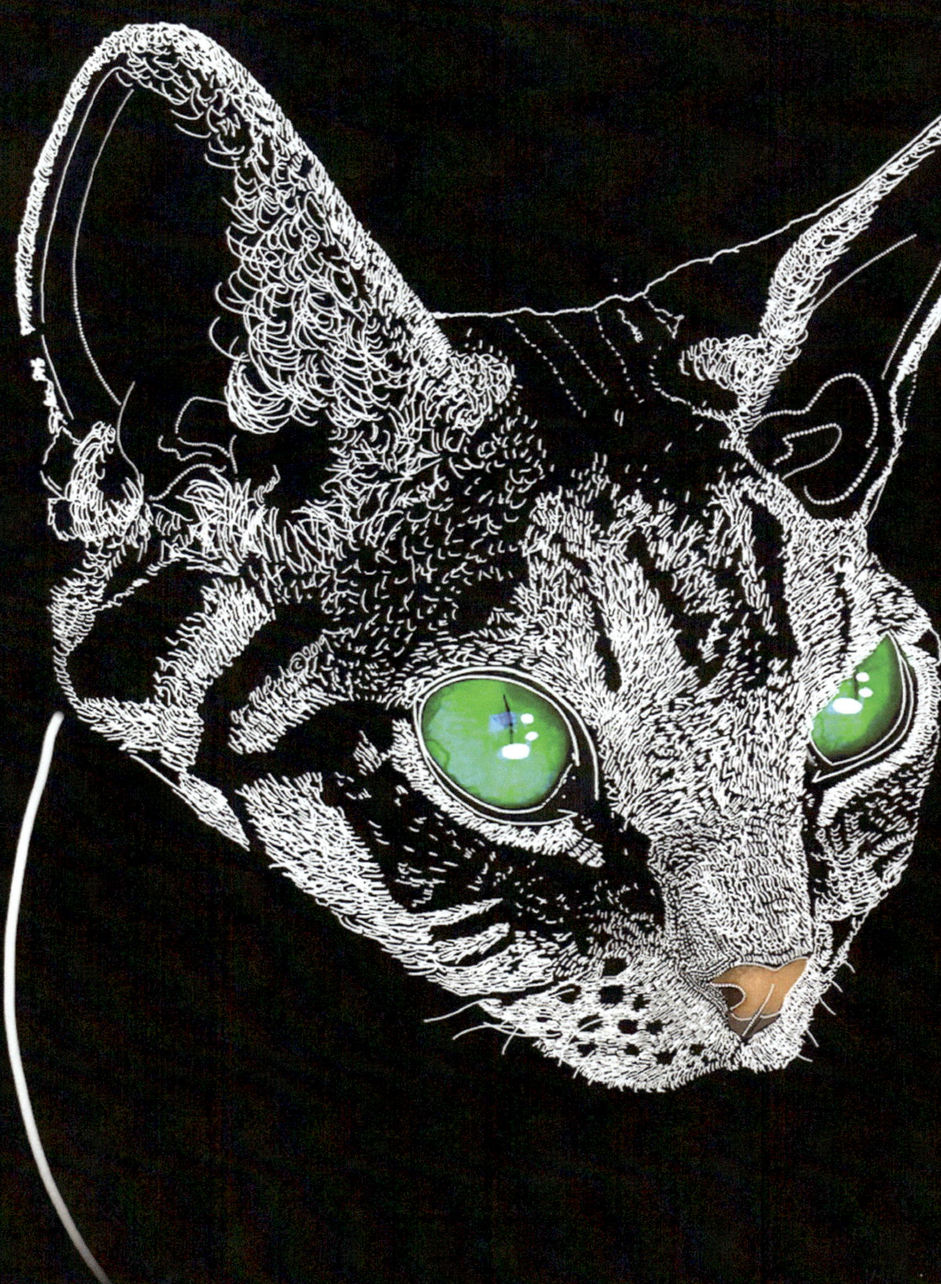

Cat Medicine

When I touch your back, my pain slips away.
Maybe for a minute, an hour, a day.
You are soft in my hand whether fur or just skin,
The touch of you and my healing begins.

Whether one or another is better or worse,
You offer me succor in the time of my curse.
Chronic's not ever going to go away.
Because of my life the pain always stay.

But when I run, I run with you.
The pain slips away when I do what you do.
While others just see a girl and a cat,
They don't know the magic of how you do that.

So jump away, run so fast, after your toy,
When you have fun, your joy is my joy.
And when we are done and settled in bed,
The pain does come back, but with much less dread.

I know it will hurt when the morning time comes.
I'm not afraid for with you I will run.
Across the house, into clouds over stars,
Away from the pain where the heaven is ours.

Art by Airie McCready

Owned

Eventually they always go
In the back of our mind we knew, we know.
Love in a body will never stay,
although we wish it was that way.
We cry and cry and miss them so,
there's so much pain in letting go.
We long for a touch, a purr, we fear
what will happen now that they are not here.
They comforted us when we were sad,
calmed us down when we were mad,
snuggled close and got so near,
when we cried they licked our tears.
The secret is, my sweet sad dears,
I'll whisper it in your deafened ears-
They were not ours, they were not yours,
we do not own the ones with paws.
They are mirrors come in feline form,
to show us things, things not the norm

We think they help, we know they love,
they are single kisses from above.
Some say angels, some say nay
-but it was supposed to be this way.
Our hearts were closed, in walls of stone-
which crumbled down once we were "owned."
Once walls fell down, the love came in,
true emotion now can begin.
Love so deep, and equal pain
come hand in paw like sun, and rain.
And though we fear it never heals,
now in good times comes what is real.
Your walls are down, defenses gone,
Your memories go on and on.
Hold out your hands to heal those,
whose little paws have flown,
and remember what a privilege it is
and was - To be so truly owned.

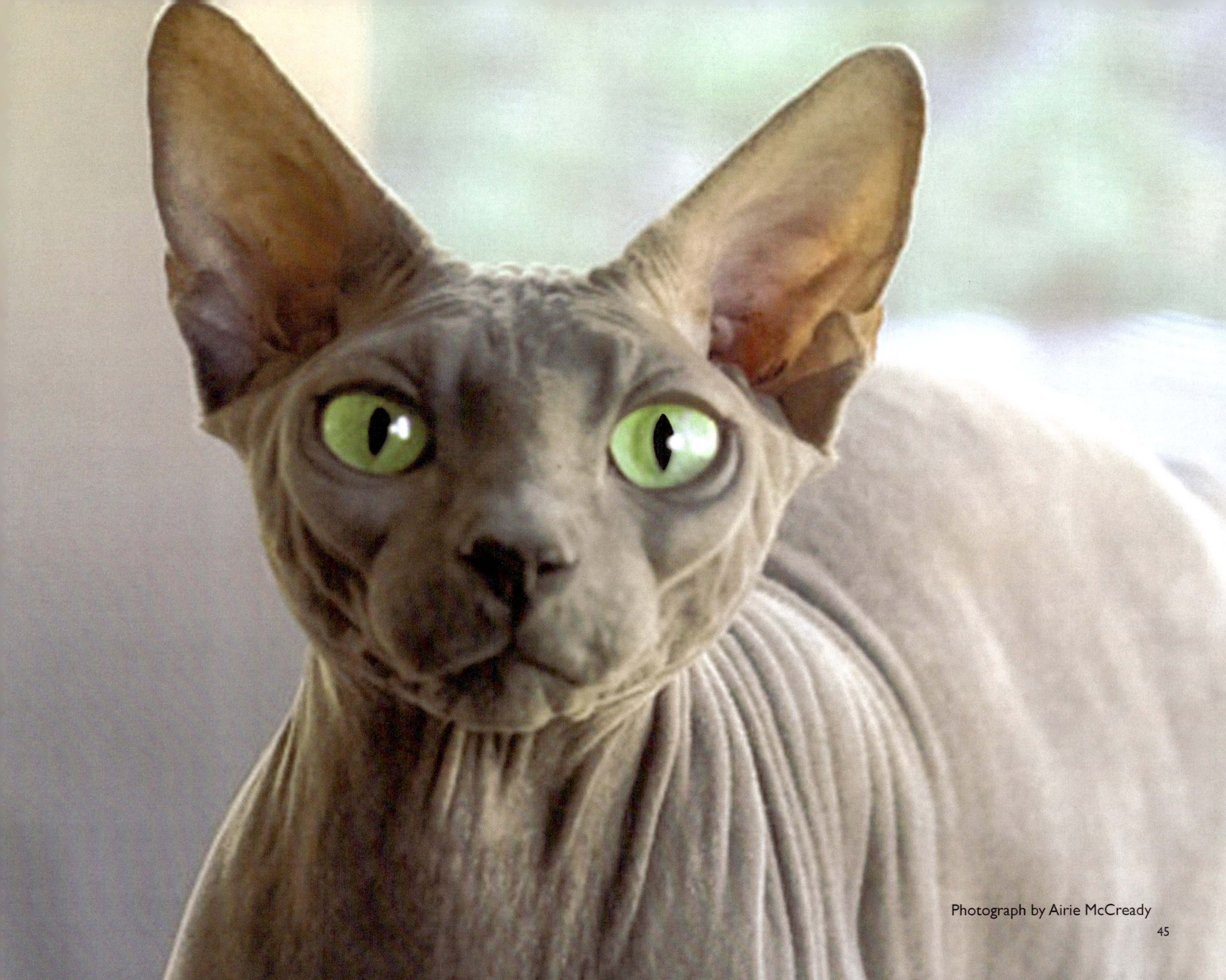

Photograph by Airie McCready

In Dreams

Sometimes, she very softly said, I think I'm crazy in the head,
I see the ghost of someone's tortoiseshell just sitting on my bed."
She tugged her long red hair and then looked through me at the hills,
Sometimes, she said, her eyes cast down,That cat, it sits there still.

When I was just a little girl, they came to me in dreams,
The people were so frightening, they made me want to scream.
The pets they were so gentle and even if they were sad,
all they ever wanted was to thank their mom's and dads.

So I struck a deal with the universe, that if they could come to me,
just the pets and not the people were the only one's I'd see.
When I was young I played with them, up and down the hall,
I'd throw, and when I turned around, there was that same red ball.

I'm older now, and they don't come so often anymore,
If I want to I can call for them, they'll walk right in my door.
But mostly I don't do it now, though they do talk to me,
If I know you, and you are sad, and they don't want you to be.

Sometimes, she said, I lay in bed, but now my dreams are soft.
I don't tell you, or him, or her, because people they have scoffed.
Sometimes, she sighed, When you have cried, and have tears no more,
I'll send them at night to give you a kiss, and softly scratch at your door.

I am, she said, not of the dead, but the dead they come to me.
I did not ask for this huge task, but what is can only be.
Goodbye, she said, with a shy smile, she walked on down the street.
I sit now still, in shock yet thrilled, for she is really me.

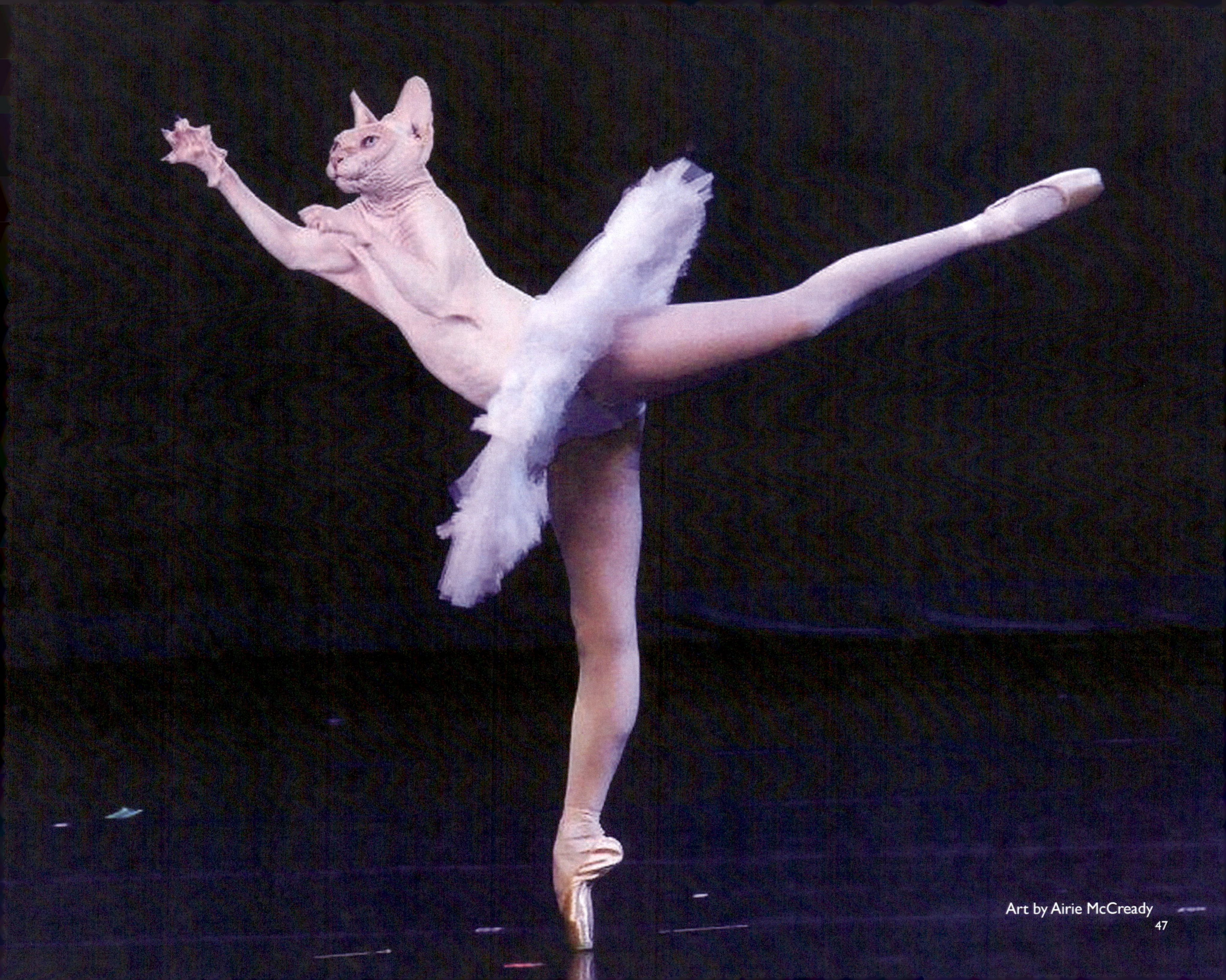
Art by Airie McCready

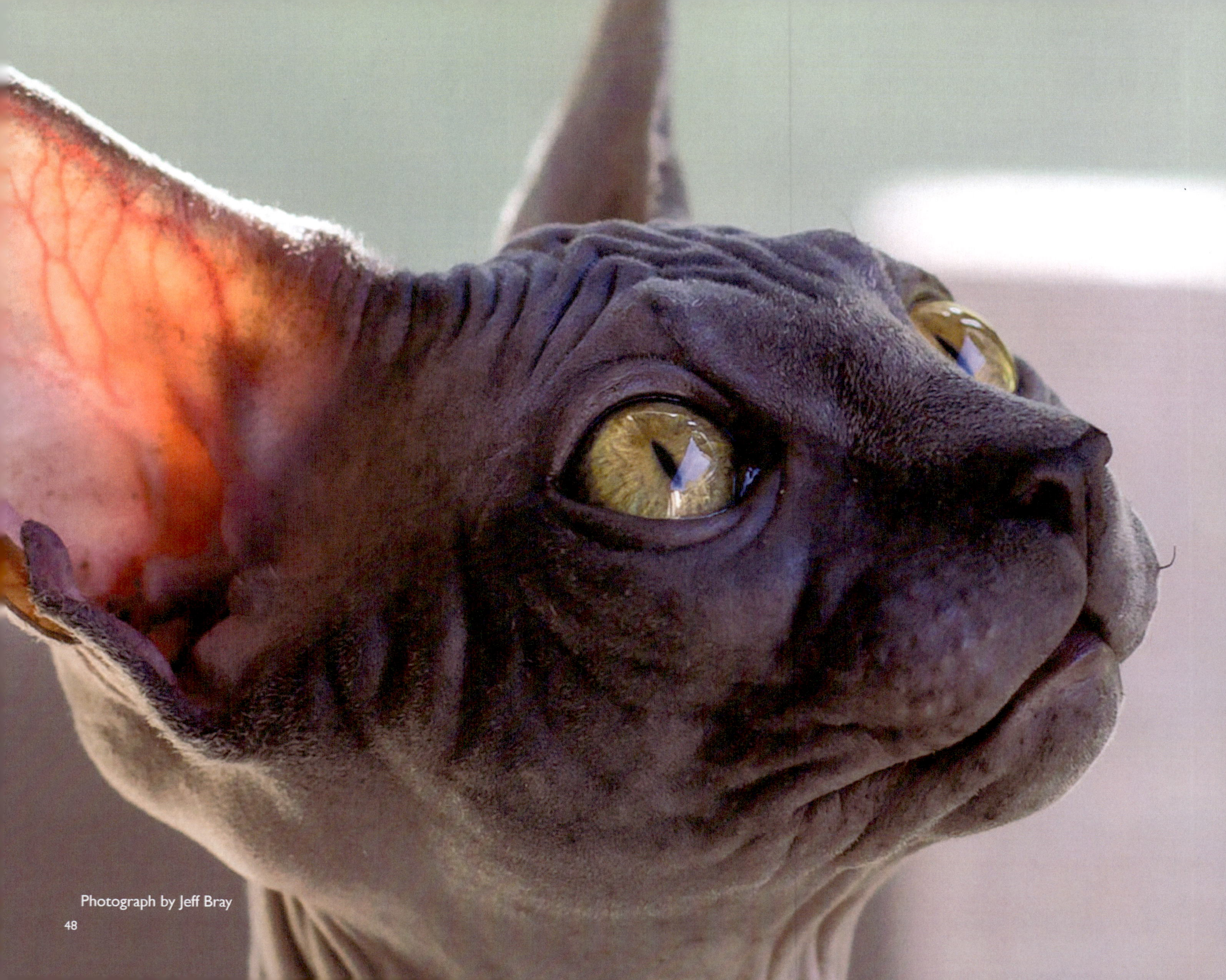

Photograph by Jeff Bray

48

Armor

At night we journey in my head, I fly with him till roads run red
With love not lust, with wine not gore, till all are happy evermore.
His mind is Christ-like, but how you say? It's focused only on the day.
The hour, the minute and not the year, in his mind there is no fear.

His shield, his armor are God made, only when natural is he afraid.
He knows not money, or what 'tis to die, just sparkling life in two big eyes.
And if he's wounded or if in pain, he does not remember that it is "again."
For the moment is all, not "it was different then," or "will this stop? And if so when?"

I am him and he is me, when in my dreams he lets me see,
I think too much, and then I wake, and worry over my mistakes.
Suffering is a human phrase, when past and future compare to craze,
paralyzed by what we think and see, and forget, most times, to just...be.

I am his and he is mine, as we travel the harder times.
Life can be cruel, or so it seems, but then, he's always in my dreams.
I woke today to see him there, on my pillow, he's tangled in my hair.
And there upon his tiny foot, a tiger-ed gauntlet with a touch of soot.

Last night we flew to the worlds end, I vanquished evil with my sword and then,
He clapped his paws and fire came, till all that needed was in flames.
And now the day-life it begins, day after day after day again.
When repetition it becomes a bore, we put on our armor and fly once more.

This Little Child

My beauty blooms when laying words like bricks from end to end.
My love it lays upon my arms with purrs that never end.
When I was small I wrote some poems, much older than I should.
When I was older I wrote some poems much better than one would.
The other kids they laughed at me alone with paper and pen.
The children they were mean to me, again and again and again.
At home I'd run and bury my face in his sweet smelling pelt,
So glad I was, that he just knew, exactly how I felt.
Meow and purr, hiss and growl, pretending I was a cat.
But I was just a little girl, and I did not like that.
So this is a poem about a poem and a little child too.
And if you have been this little child, I send my love to you.

Photograph by Jeff Bra

Acknowlegement

Special thanks to all my cats, whether naked or furred, still on this plane or crossed over to another, gods and goddesses, who have guided and taught me on this journey, so I may deeply understand them and share some of these teachings with you.

To Devlin and Sansa, my heart cat and soul cat, without them I would be lost. To my One True North, who is now a giant naked cat. To my gallant Rhys and his My LadyPants. Each of them has taught me so much.

Thanks to my Facebook family, who always encouraged me to do this book, and let me know if my writing resonated with them. They turned to me in their times of need with their own cats. Learning often comes through pain, not just joy, and they shared both with me.

And last, but not least, to my longtime friend and publisher, Mandy Parrey. She came along at a time when I was drifting and helped me refocus and get back on track.

About the Author

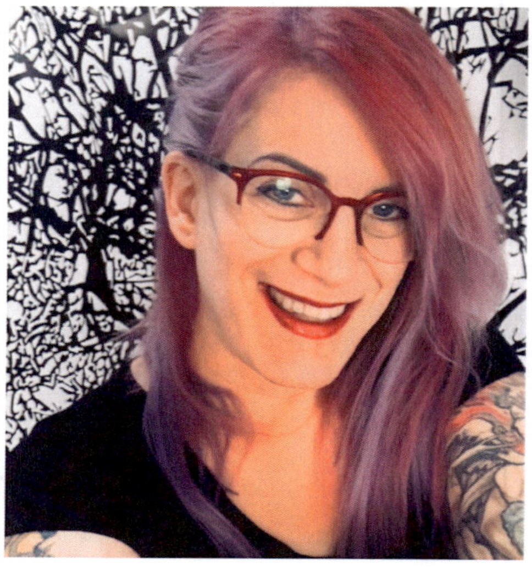

Airie McCready, after earning her journalism degree, took an unconventional path. Instead of journalism, she immersed herself in fine art, computer graphics, and freelancing as an art director. After her marriage ended, she adopted a new name to shed her ex-husband's shadow. This marked the beginning of her self-discovery journey, leading her to help people understand the profound love and companionship cats offer. Driven by her passion for teaching, McCready has become an expert in Sphynx and Devon Rex cat behavior, believing her deep connection with her felines is both physical and spiritual.

About her writing, she states, "The joy of a new kitten or cat releases emotions that make me tumble deep down to see who that kitten is on an energetic level as well as how they fit into our world as they grow up. Later, the loss of a beloved member of my feline family triggers what I have learned and what needs to be let go and grieved. Caught in a Cat Romance expresses the polarity of love and grief that any pet lover can understand."